THE 49'ERS

The Story of the California Gold Rush

James Marshall's discovery of gold at Sutter's mill, in California, in 1848 was a clarion call that rang throughout the nation, inspiring dreams of fabulous wealth in men from every walk of life. The result was a virtual stampede to the gold fields, nearly two hundred thousand men in two years. They battled every hardship known to man, dug fortunes from the earth, built cities overnight, performed heroic acts and infamous crimes, and changed forever the frontier life of that remote land. This story chronicles the deeds of those men and shows how they influenced the course of American expansion. It also reveals the qualities that have given shape to the American character: the humor and resourcefulness, the ability to overcome seemingly insurmountable obstacles, the passionate dream of success and riches, the desire for order and justice.

Books by Bob and Jan Young

ACROSS THE TRACKS

THE 49'ERS: The Story of the California Gold Rush

GOOD-BYE, AMIGOS

ONE SMALL VOICE

PLANT DETECTIVE: David Douglas

SUNDAY DREAMER

THE 49'ERS

The Story of the California Gold Rush

by

BOB and JAN YOUNG

Maps and Drawings by
BARRY MARTIN

JULIAN MESSNER
NEW YORK

Published simultaneously in the United States and Canada by
Julian Messner, a division of Simon & Schuster, Inc.,
1 West 39 Street, New York, N.Y. 10018.

Second Printing, 1967

Printed in the United States of America
Library of Congress Catalog Card No. 66-13999

DEDICATION

For
Don A. Allen, Sr., member of the California Assembly
and
Allan R. Ottley, of the California State Library
In recognition of their appreciation of Californiana.

Contents

I

"Boys, We've Found a Gold Mine!"

JANUARY 24, 1848, BEGAN LIKE ANY OTHER DAY IN the Sierra foothills, crisp, crystal clear, the air dazzling with that golden light so peculiar to California mornings. Though it was only seven thirty, already the sunlight sifted in splintered shafts through the tall, ponderosa pines and laid a jeweled blanket across the waters of the American River.

James Wilson Marshall stepped outside his cabin and drew a satisfied breath of the pine-scented air. Imagine, late January and weather like this: Not much like the snows of New Jersey or the rains in Oregon. By George, he liked this new home!

Leaving the cabin, he followed a well-trod path that led toward the river, where he and his men would be starting to work in another hour. There was good reason for that feeling of satisfaction as he looked at the unfinished skeleton of the new mill already raised against the sky. Thanks to his friend John Sutter, his days of wandering were over and he was launched in a business of his own. "James Marshall, mill-owner and lumberman." That had a nice ring!

Mustered out of the army the previous April, Marshall, like many others who had fought to win California, had sought out John Sutter hoping to find employment. Instead, Sutter had offered him a partnership in a lumber mill. Badly in need of the lumber for the extensive building going on at his fort at the junction of the Sacramento and American rivers, Sutter had offered to put up the land, timber and supplies if Marshall would contribute his skill and managership in building and running the mill. To the thirty-six-year-old Marshall it had come as the chance of a lifetime.

It had taken him a while to select exactly the right site on the South Fork of the American River in the beautiful Coloma Valley, but by August he had construction under way, with the help of about a dozen men, most of them former soldiers like himself. One, Peter Weimer, had brought his family along so that his wife could do their cooking.

By December with the help of friendly Indians they had their log houses built and the framework of the mill erected. After that had come seven weeks' work on the brush dam for the millpond. Now, their attention had turned to the millrace. Marshall surveyed the partially dug channel that would carry the swift flow of water to power the mill. The location of the race had been in his mind when he had selected this site. All that had been necessary was to have his men deepen an old dry channel of the river, which already cut across the sandbar behind the mill.

By now work was progressing so well that Marshall spent his days building the machinery that would go into the mill, while his helpers, lacking his skill as a millwright, carried on the excavation work alone.

Each evening Marshall inspected the men's work, then raised the wooden gates at the end of the millrace and let the water surge through the channel to wash away any loose rock and gravel that had fallen in during the day. The water ran all night. In the morning before he joined the others at breakfast, Marshall returned and closed the gates again in preparation for the day's work. As the water drained away, he walked along the drying channel marking those places where he must instruct Peter Weimer to have the Indians dig deeper.

This morning as usual, Marshall paused for a moment looking across the sun-dappled waters and surveying the dark line of the race before he bent and closed the wooden gates. Except for his rather brooding, sultry, dark eyes, there was nothing particularly distinguished about his looks. Like most California men of that day he wore a beard. His clothes were typical of the California way of life. On his legs and feet were the buckskin leggings and moccasins of the woodsman. His flannel frontier shirt and linen trousers were those of the Yankee, while perched atop his head was a Mexican sombrero.

"Lumberman and millowner," he repeated the words aloud. They had a pleasant ring of stability.

With a start, Marshall brought himself back to reality as he saw that the water cut off by the closed gates was lowering rapidly in the channel. He set out in quick, sure strides along the millrace to complete his inspection. Water dropped from two feet to less than one. Something glittering caught his eye. Dipping a hand into the shrinking stream, he brought up a pebble and revolved it slowly in his fingers.

A sudden pounding began in his chest. The pebble was the same size and shape as a pea. It had a strange brassy color.

He spotted another in the few remaining inches of water and scooped it up too. By George, it looked like gold! But he couldn't be sure. The only gold ore he had ever seen had a slightly reddish caste. It could be iron pyrite, fool's gold.

He licked the pebble and noticed a biting, metal taste, but that could be characteristic of many ores. Finally, he laid one of the pebbles on a flat rock and hammered it with a stone.

The pounding of his heart leaped to match the movement of his muscular arms. The pebble was soft . . . it was malleable . . . already it had been flattened into a flake . . . !

It was customary for Marshall to go every morning to close the millrace, but ordinarily he did not linger so long. Mrs.

Weimer, who had a sharp temper so early in the morning, was growing impatient about her cooling breakfast. Pete Weimer went outside to look for his boss, followed by Henry Bigler and Charlie Bennett.

Marshall came hurrying toward them from the race, holding something in his battered white sombrero. "Boys, I think we've found a gold mine!"

The mouths of the three men dropped open as though controlled by the same invisible wire, but moments later they were exchanging questioning looks. Marshall's ringing voice had reached into the cabin. Scraping and thumping, the rest of the men rushed from the breakfast table.

Yet as Weimer, Bennett, William Scott and the younger men gathered around Marshall their faces continued to be curious but skeptical. All were well enough acquainted with their leader to know his strange, sometimes inexplicable moods. He could be pulling a joke. It could also be some wild figment of his imagination. Not one of them was certain that he could recognize gold if he saw it.

"It certainly glitters," Weimer admitted, then shook his head. "But couldn't it be iron or maybe bits of copper?" As second in command, he was the only one with courage to question Marshall's statement.

Someone brought a hammer and they repeated the test. "By gosh, it doesn't shatter." Henry Bigler began to catch some of Marshall's enthusiasm now.

Azariah Smith dug into his pocket to produce a five-dollar gold piece and compared it with the flakes for color. "It's similar but not exactly the same," he said.

"That could be because of the alloy in the coin," Weimer put in, more willing to believe now.

He borrowed one of his wife's pots. While the two young Weimer boys peered round-eyed over the top, the men boiled some of the flakes with a bit of the potash Mrs. Weimer used for making soap. When removed, the flakes still retained their luster, yet all knew these simple tests were inconclusive. They wanted to believe but the skepticism still remained. Someone voiced the thoughts of all.

"If it really is gold, how come no one else ever discovered it before? There can't be much of it."

The men went about their work as usual that day, but Marshall stopped frequently to join them at the millrace, showing more interest in the digging operations than he ever had before. In the now-dry channel and on some of the piles of excavated earth he picked up more particles. Finally, he sent one of the Indians to borrow a flat pan from Mrs. Weimer. Shaking some of the silt in the water-filled tin he watched as the glittering flakes settled to the bottom. Now, a few of the other men stooped occasionally to pick up the strange flakes.

By evening Marshall had quite a collection of the particles, which he wrapped in a cloth for safekeeping. The following day he found more. For several nights he was unable to sleep, wondering if he had indeed found gold. Each night as they let water run through the race he kept thinking that the last of the particles might wash away and disappear, but each morning they found more.

Finally Marshall realized that he could wait no longer. After breakfast, he gathered his men around him. "Boys, we've got to know the truth of this thing. Captain Sutter may laugh at us, but I'm going to the fort and show him what we've found."

Behind him the men were nodding. By now every one of them had a small collection of his own. As he took the reins of his horse, Marshall swung back. "I guess I don't have to ask you to keep this thing quiet until I return."

The men needed no warning. Every hand went up in an oath of secrecy. With a few last words to Weimer about the work to be done in his absence, Marshall mounted his horse and disappeared into the forest.

As he trotted southward alone, sometimes beside the glistening waters of the river, or through the musky incense of stands of pines, his mind was in a turmoil. Hadn't he seen with his own eyes that the gold was practically unlimited? He could become the wealthiest man in all California. Mill-owner indeed! Sutter might very well make him a full partner in all of his enterprises. Suddenly wild, wonderful dreams tumbled one upon another through his mind. In his excitement he did not notice that it had begun to rain and he was getting soaked to the skin.

It was January 28 when Marshall drew up his dripping horse beside the adobe walls of Sutter's Fort. His dark eyes feverish, his wet shirt plastered to his muscular back and his battered sombrero askew and cascading water, he burst into Sutter's office.

Sutter, a short but impressive-looking man, dressed in a frock coat and with his beard fastidiously trimmed, looked up in astonishment.

"Captain . . . Captain Sutter, I must speak to you immediately . . . and alone." In his excitement Marshall could hardly stammer out the words, but his eyes darted meaningfully to a clerk at work at a corner desk.

Puzzled but agreeable, since he knew Marshall to be a thoroughly honest and likable though somewhat peculiar man, Sutter nodded to his clerk to go on with his work and led the way into his private rooms.

"Lock the door," Marshall ordered in a harsh voice. Indulgently Sutter obeyed.

"Now bring me scales and a basin of water," Marshall demanded. Growing more puzzled by the moment, Sutter opened the door again and gave the order to the clerk. When he turned around, Marshall had laid a folded white cloth on the table. Opening it, he displayed the glittering particles. "Captain, I think I have discovered gold," he said.

Sutter's eyes widened. He picked up one of the larger particles about the size of a small pea. Others diminished in size to little more than grains of dust. When Sutter's clerk appeared suddenly in the doorway with the scales and basin of water, Marshall hastily thrust the packet back into his pocket. This time when the clerk had gone, Sutter did not have to be reminded to lock the door behind him.

"Is it gold?" Marshall asked.

"I do not know," Sutter admitted honestly, "but it looks like it. There are some tests we can make."

For several hours the men remained locked in the room testing the particles. Sutter consulted an encyclopedia. They pounded the grains again for malleability. They weighed the gold against some silver coins, both in the air and in water. When the scales with the silver were lowered into the basin, they floated while the side with the gold sank to the bottom. They tested the particles with acid. Finally when they had exhausted every test that Sutter knew, he said in a strangely awed voice, "I am convinced that it is gold."

The gleam returned to Marshall's eyes. "We're rich, Captain Sutter! Wait till I tell the boys . . ."

Sutter was astute enough to forsee the possibilities of this find. He caught Marshall's arm. "We must act with caution, Jim. For the time being we must keep this secret."

For all his wild dreams, Marshall was no fool. "Don't worry about me, Captain. I won't let the secret out, or my boys either. I swore them to secrecy before I left."

"Good," Sutter said. "I want to have a look at that millrace myself, but to go rushing out of here today, especially in the face of this storm, would tell everyone something was afoot. I'll take care of a few business matters, then be along as quickly as possible as though I was making a routine visit."

Marshall was so anxious to return to his men with the good news that he refused Sutter's invitation to spend the night. Before he remounted for the trip home, he and Sutter clasped hands again and repeated their vow of secrecy. Marshall whipped up his fresh mount. Minutes later, he was swallowed in the gray curtain of rain.

II

Fortune Hunters All

GOLD, AU ACCORDING TO THE METALLURGIST. "A heavy, yellow metallic chemical with a high degree of ductility and malleability," according to Webster's dictionary. Gold, symbol of riches and wealth, the life blood of nations.

During the sixteenth century Spain dominated the world because of that one magic word. Columbus, sailing under the Spanish flag, had pioneered the way in the New World for the colonies that were to make Spain rich. By 1540 the wealth found by Cortez in Mexico and by Pizarro in Peru was already pouring back across the Atlantic. Mexico had been conquered, colonization had begun and, pushing seaward from the Pacific Coast, Cortez had discovered Baja or Lower California, which he and other Spaniards of that day mistook for a long, barren island laying off the Mexican coast. Yet Spain was not satisfied with the gold that already filled her coffers. She continued to search for the mythical Straits of Anian which were supposed to link North America with the even greater wealth of the Orient.

On September 28, 1542, under a darkening sky, two small ships scudded helplessly ahead of a mounting Pacific storm. They were tiny vessels, so small they were built without decks, and crudely constructed with iron fittings that had been carried across Mexico from the Atlantic to shipyards on the west coast. It was impossible to outrace the building waves. Soon the tiny ships were being tossed like eggshells, one moment shooting ahead, the next skidding sidewise, occasionally shuddering back to the surface as waves broke over them.

"Land, land ahead!" a sailor in the lead ship suddenly gave the welcome cry. Juan Rodriguez Cabrillo, the leader of the expedition who had been straining to keep track of their struggling sister vessel, turned to follow the sailor's pointing finger. Ahead, barely visible through the clouds, he saw a rising black bulk of land and motioned to the helmsman to set a new course.

Moments later the cries of relief turned to alarm. What at first had appeared to be a headland now proved no more than a jagged island of rock rising from the sea, and some gigantic current was dragging them directly toward the towering cliffs. Minutes from what seemed like destruction, the little craft wallowed free from the grasp of the current and the rock shot behind them.

"Land ahead!" the cry rang again. Now another great rocky island loomed on the other side of them, and again they were grabbed by the current and carried so perilously close that even above the roar of the storm they could hear the barking of the great herds of sea lions on the island's rocky shelves. They passed still another island where great clouds of sea gulls rose into the air.

"Land ahead!" This time the cry brought little response, everyone believing the lookout had spotted still another of the treacherous islands. Then a sudden silence fell over them. In one of those miraculous moments of calm that appear sometimes in Pacific storms, the sea had quieted and the clouds had parted. Ahead bathed in sunlight, they saw the glistening white sands of a long, flat spit of land, farther north the dark headlands of a point, and between the two, what appeared to be the narrow entrance to a harbor.

Cabrillo let out a grateful cry and crossed himself. His men, who moments before had been praying for salvation, did the same. A short time later both small ships had slipped safely into a large and quiet harbor. Outside the entrance, the storm closed in and raged again, but within, the blue waters were still and the sun shone on the surrounding oak-dotted hills. Cabrillo would put down in his diary that it was a land of perpetual summer, and that very same day he went ashore and took possession of it in the name of the king of Spain, the first Spaniard to land on the soil of present-day California.

The islands through which Cabrillo had just sailed were the rocky Coronados which lie off the coast of Mexico almost on the boundary line with the United States. The beckoning bay that had offered shelter from the storm was San Diego Harbor.

For several days the two ships waited out the storm in the harbor. The sailors would have liked to remain longer after their arduous three months at sea, but their mission had barely begun. Juan Cabrillo, like a number of other navigators who sailed for Spain, was Portuguese by birth. His expedition was one of three sent out from the west coast of Mexico in 1542 in an attempt to discover the Straits of Anian. The first expedition was to explore the Gulf of California. The second, under Cabrillo, was to round the tip of Lower California and sail north up the Pacific Coast. The third was to head directly west into the Pacific Ocean.

The day after their arrival, three of Cabrillo's men were wounded by arrows fired by the Indians while they were fishing. The wounds were slight, the arrows being of very inferior quality. Cabrillo quickly determined that they had been fired more in fear than anger, and as soon as he showed the Indians that he was not angry and offered them gifts, they became friends.

Continuing up the coast, he stopped several times to make more friends among the Indians and explore the offshore Channel Islands. Finally driven back by bad weather, his two vessels sought shelter in the lee of the island of San Miguel.

Here Cabrillo fell and broke his arm. It was a serious break near the shoulder, yet in spite of his pain, he refused to consider his crew's suggestion that they turn back. In fact, with a favorable change of winds, he insisted on sailing north again. High seas and rocky cliffs kept them from landing, but they sighted a bay lined with pines, probably Montery, before the weather forced them back to San Miguel.

By now Cabrillo burned with fever from the spreading infection in his arm. In January of 1543 he died surrounded by his grieving men. On his deathbed he extracted a promise that they would go on.

"Sail north, sail north, Bartolomeo," he pleaded in his failing voice. "Do not let our struggles be a failure."

Bartolomeo Ferrelo, next in command, gave his solemn promise to continue. The sailors buried Cabrillo on the island, little more than a great rock rising from the sea, swept almost bare of vegetation by constant winds and swirling sands. Before they sailed on, shifting sands were already obliterating the lonely grave.

Ferrelo tried to carry out his promise. He sailed north again, but as before he could not land and dangerous winds and tides buffeted him far out to sea. Finally bad weather and dwindling supplies forced him and the survivors of the expedition back to Mexico, where he turned in Cabrillo's reports on friendly Indians and the quiet harbor of San Diego with its days of perpetual summer.

Spain had little interest in a land of endless summer. Cabrillo's discoveries were completely eclipsed by the success of the third expedition which had sailed west into the Pacific. It had reached the Philippine Islands. Spain had her trade route to the Orient at last, and the era of the great Manila galleons was about to begin!

For the next two hundred years Alta or Upper California was almost forgotten. On their homeward journey the Manila galleons sometimes stopped along the coast to take on water or to make repairs. Some of the galleon masters were commissioned to make maps of the coastline but even these orders were more concerned with the galleons' safety than any plan for settlement.

It was natural that other nations should envy Spain's riches. Lacking gold themselves, they turned to the next best thing, robbing Spain of hers. The Caribbean Sea became the hideout for vessels of all types who preyed on the Spanish treasure ships as they plied their way across the Atlantic. Some of the vessels openly flew the ensigns of pirates; others were freebooters working under the flags of rival nations. Francis Drake, sailing under the English flag, belonged to the latter group. In 1577 after a successful tour of the Caribbean, Drake with his ship the *Golden Hinde* and four other vessels was commissioned to sail through the Straits of Magellan and across the Pacific to try and find some new trade routes for England.

Once safely at sea, Drake announced the additional goal of piracy. When one member of his crew protested, he was promptly hanged and that served to end further argument. Before the little fleet had completed its voyage down the east coast of South America, Drake had seized so much loot that all but one of his treasure-laden vessels had to be sent back to England.

Until Drake came through the Straits of Magellan in 1578, the Pacific had been Spain's private sea; but the fact that he had only the *Golden Hinde* left did not stop him from sweeping up the South American coast taking treasure along the way. By the time he reached the waters off the coast of Mexico he had no choice but to continue around the world. Rounding the Horn he had caught his enemies unaware, but by now the alerted Spanish would be laying in wait for him if he attempted to return over the same route.

To prepare for the perilous journey across the Pacific, he sailed north along the isolated coast of Alta California. In a small bay north of San Francisco he took shelter for a month during 1579 while he repaired his ship. Raising the English flag, he paved the way for England's future claim to the Pacific Coast; then he continued on to become the first Englishman to circumnavigate the globe.

The defeat of the Spanish Amada in 1588 marked the end of Spain's supremacy of the seas, though her colonial might would not crumble for another two centuries. However, during those ensuing years other countries began to rise as colonial powers too. By 1760, the thirteen English colonies were flourishing on the Atlantic seaboard, and Russian fur traders had crossed the Bering Straits and moved into the Aleutians. Spain, herself, had pushed her Mexican frontier north into what is now Arizona, New Mexico and Texas, which seemed enough to deter the English. It was largely to thwart the Russian advance that Spain decided in 1769 the time had come to occupy Alta California.

The little band of men struggling north through the arid wastelands of Baja California presented an incongruous sight. Blistering sunlight reflected from the metal helmets and the leather armor of more than a dozen armed and mounted soldiers. At their lead rode Gaspar de Portola, a darkly handsome man and military governor of the province of Baja California. Walking beside him was a stocky, brown-robed, Franciscan father, supporting himself on a knotted cane and limping painfully with each step. Next came an assortment of servants and muleteers, most dressed in the flat brimmed hats and leather chaps of the vaqueros of that day, while still farther behind straggled a motley collection of Christianized Indians, some dressed in cast-off clothing, others almost naked, having tossed away their uncomfortable garments in the heat.

Though the party was traveling in the tracks of another band that had preceded them, they had suffered many hardships since leaving the last mission outpost in Baja California. The country was dry and rugged, carved by jagged canyons and sprinkled with savage cactus. Even the scanty vegetation was baked brown by a burning June sun. They had been attacked by unfriendly Indians, gone without water, and already more than half the Christianized Indians they were bringing with them to help convert the natives of California had either died or deserted.

Of particular concern to everyone was Father Junípero Serra, head of the Franciscan missionaries in California. He was gray-haired and no longer young. The miles of rugged trail had opened an old sore on his leg, so that every step seemed agony, yet he refused to ride or accept medical care. Like other Franciscans of his time Father Serra believed that the more earthly sufferings he endured, the greater the proof of his service to God. However, that night as they made camp in a rocky draw, the day's walk had been so difficult that he finally accepted treatment of his leg.

He allowed one of the muleteers to rub it with some of the same evil-smelling ointment that he used on the animals. "Father, I am afraid. I do not believe we will live to reach our new home," the man confided as he knelt at the friar's feet, massaging his leg.

"There is nothing to fear, my son," Father Serra reassured him. "We do not have much farther to go. Our brothers who have gone ahead already will have started our new settlement for us. We have made our plans well."

Father Serra was right. Once the decision had been made to occupy Alta California the plans of the Sacred Expeditions, as they were called, had been made with the thoroughness of a military manuever. This was no simple plan to build a single outpost; men and equipment were being sent to occupy five hundred miles of coastline. To accomplish their goal they were traveling in five separate expeditions, three by sea and two by land.

The Missions

In February of 1769, the *San Carlos* had set sail, carrying the heavy equipment and altar furniture along with Lieutenant Pedro Fages, who was to be the new colony's military governor, and his company of soldiers. A month later, the *San Antonio* had followed with more men and supplies. In March, the first land party under Captain Fernando Rivera, with more soldiers, cattle and a band of Indian converts, had started north up the peninsula of Baja California. In May, Portola, leader of the combined expeditions, followed with Father Serra and the second land party, while a third ship, the *San Jose,* set sail with additional food supplies. Portola's orders called for the founding of a presidio and mission at San Diego and another presidio and mission almost five hundred miles north at Monterey. After that Father Serra would be left to found more missions in between as he saw fit. It was an ambitious enterprise, but much care had gone into the preparations.

The muleteer seemed comforted by Father Serra's assurances. In the morning the father's leg was so much improved that he did not slow them at all that day.

Those next days they continued up the arid peninsula losing more animals and Indian converts along the way: out of the forty-four Indians who had started with them, finally only twelve remained. On the last day of June they came out on the top of a flat, table mountain and saw in the distance the long white strand, the dark point and blue waters of San Diego Bay.

The next day they started around the bay. Cheers went up from the soldiers and muleteers as they caught sight of the two Spanish vessels laying at anchor. Even Portola and the father exchanged smiles, but as they drew closer Father Serra's face became puzzled. The ships seemed strangely still and deserted. His eyes searched vainly ahead for the activity of several hundred men, for the buildings that by now should be half-erected, for the huge piles of stores that should have been carried ashore from the ships.

Beside him, Portola seemed to share his misgivings. Where was everyone? Why had no party come out to greet them? In response to the gunfire of his soldiers, they heard a feeble answering salute; then a small greeting party came toward them. It had almost reached them before they recognized Lieutenant Fages, so emaciated his eyes were like two dark holes burned in a masklike face. Behind him Captain Rivera was almost as gaunt, the welcoming soldiers little more than skeletons.

Ahead, Father Serra saw the settlement now, if one could call it a settlement—crude brush shelters protecting scores of men who lay on the ground wrapped in blankets; pitifully small pile of stores at the water's edge; farther back at the foot of the cliffs, the telltale crosses of a cemetery where even now two soldiers were digging. It was not a settlement—it was a camp of death!

The story Fages and Rivera had to tell was harrowing. The *San Antonio* had been the first to arrive, everyone aboard sick and disabled with scurvy. The *San Carlos,* which had started a whole month earlier but had been blown off course, had not arrived until three weeks later. All of her crew except two were dead. By some miracle Lieutenant Fages and his landlubber soldiers had been able to maneuver the ship into the harbor, though most of them were barely able to stand. Rivera and his land party had arrived next, having lost most of their cattle and Indians on the trail. Their condition had been nothing compared to that of the sea parties. Immediately they had turned to caring for the sick and dying. In spite of their efforts, sixty graves had been dug below the cliffs. As for the third ship, the *San Jose,* it was never to appear, having been lost at sea with all hands. Of more than 300 men who had set out, only 126 remained.

Father Serra, Portola and even the frightened muleteer

forgot their own miseries as they turned to caring for the sick and unloading the ships. On July 9, the *San Antonio,* manned by only nine sailors, all that were well enough to sail, started back to Mexico for help. On July 14, Portola with Fages, Rivera and the soldiers who were able to travel started north to found the second settlement at Monterey. Two days after he left, Father Serra took time off from his nursing duties to raise a cross and formally dedicate his first mission, San Diego de Alcalá.

It was January before Portola returned. His mission had been a failure, for he had not been able to locate Monterey Bay. However, traveling farther north he had found the great bay of San Francisco, hitherto undiscovered because earlier explorers had failed to spot its narrow fog-shrouded entrance from the sea. Running short of supplies, Portola and his men had made it back to San Diego only by slaughtering and eating one of their stringy mules each night.

At San Diego, things were little better. The *San Antonio* had failed to return. With her tiny crew there was a chance she had never reached Mexico. Corn planted by the fathers had been picked out by the birds. The men were existing on a diet of fish with an occasional wild goose. Some of the soldiers already had traded most of their clothing to the Indians for food. Reunited, the party began a lonely vigil by the sea, but weeks passed with no sign of the ship.

In mid-March Portola and Father Serra held a conference. "If help does not reach us by the end of the month, we must pack what we can carry and try to make our way back to the missions in Baja California," Portola said.

Founding the California missions had become Father Serra's sole objective. "I cannot believe that God would send us on this long journey to have us fail. I cannot believe that those who died did not go to their martyrdom without some cause," he insisted.

With his fellow friars, Father Serra began a nine-day

novena of prayers. On March 23, only days before the deadline set by Portola, the tiny presidio was alerted by a shout from the lookout. "A sail! A sail!" the cry raced from one man to another.

The following morning the *San Antonio* dropped anchor in the bay, her holds bulging with the food and supplies to save the colony. Later that spring a combined land and sea expedition went north to successfully found the second presidio and mission at Monterey. His work completed, Portola returned to Mexico, leaving Father Serra and his brothers to found three more missions during the next five years.

By now the Spaniards had learned a great deal more about the geography of California. They knew of the two great mountain ranges that ran its length: the gentle Coastal Range that hugged the 750 miles of curving coastline, and inland, farther to the east, the towering, perpetually snow-clad Sierra Nevadas. Lying between these two ranges down the very middle of the state was the great Central Valley, closed off at the south above Los Angeles and at the north below the Oregon border where the ranges curved together. However, the Spaniards did not know yet that this great interior valley was drained by two large rivers, the Sacramento from the north and the San Joaquin from the south, which joined to empty into San Francisco Bay. They did not know either what lay beyond the mountains to the east. They knew only that earlier explorers pushing north from Mexico claimed it was a great impassable desert. In founding the first settlements, Portola and Father Serra had discovered something that the Americans would still find true almost a century later—for all her golden promise, California was an almost inaccessible land to reach. Guarded by treacherous Pacific currents on the west, mountains and deserts to the east, she was as isolated from the rest of the world as though she had remained that island shown on the early maps. It was an isolation that would effect the course of her history for the next century.

On the Atlantic Coast the Thirteen Colonies were ready to launch their successful struggle for freedom. On the Pacific Coast, the two presidios and five missions of Spain struggled merely to stay alive. Dependent on the irregular supply ships that buffeted their way up the coast from Mexico, friars and soldiers lived constantly on the verge of starvation. For centuries Spain had followed a colonial policy of advancing by priest and soldier. In California, it was evident this policy must be changed. To hold the new land, permanent settlers, farmers, families and cattle herds must be brought into make the settlements self-sustaining. But how were they to get them there? To bring them by sea was impossible. To take them by ship to Baja California then up the long peninsula was impractical. To bring them directly from the mainland could not be done because of the impassable desert.

Juan Bautista de Anza, Mexico's leading Apache fighter and commander of the remote frontier post of Tubac in the state of Sonora, Mexico, did not share this opinion. He did not believe that any desert was impassable. In 1774 accompanied by Friar Francisco Garces and a party of soldiers, Anza set out from Tubac, which today lies just across the border in Arizona, to cross the formidable Colorado River, the treacherous sands of the desert, and reach California overland. That his men almost perished in the sand dunes and arrived at the San Gabriel Mission with many walking afoot did not bother Anza. Barely waiting to reassure Father Serra that help was on the way, he rushed back to Mexico over the same route.

Two years later he returned. This time Anza brought with him 240 men, women and children, 695 horses and mules and 355 head of cattle in one of the most incredible mass migrations ever recorded. These families did not travel by wagon.

They rode horseback, the entire distance, many coming as far as two thousand miles from the interior of Mexico. They slept on the ground, often went without water, nearly froze crossing the desert, lost a good portion of their horses and cattle, yet arrived in California a larger band than when they had started, for three babies were born along the way. There was only one death, a woman dying in childbirth their first night out. Having escorted them safely to Monterey, Anza went on to select the site for their new home on San Francisco Bay, for these were the hardy pioneers who were to found the little village of Yerba Buena that would later become San Francisco.

Before returning to Mexico, Anza completed one last mission for his government. He explored the far shoreline of the great bay to see if it was fed by a river. With a small group of soldiers and Father Font, his diarist and spiritual adviser, he traveled far enough up the bay to reach a point where the water turned from salt to fresh.

Anza drank with satisfaction and wiped a drop from his dark, pointed beard. "It must be a river, Father, the water is fresh," he said.

Father Font, always the austere perfectionist, tightened his thin lips. "That is no proof. How can it be a river when there is no debris along the banks such as would wash down during spring flood season?" He pointed across the sparkling water. "How can it be a river when there is no current?"

"Perhaps there is a current but we cannot see it." Anza ordered two of the soldiers to toss a log into the water. Instead of floating downstream it slowly bobbed back to shore.

"See," Father Font pursued relentlessly. "It is not a river but a great, fresh water lake. Look at how blue and clear it is and how wide. Look at the little waves that lap on the shore. Believe me I know about these things."

Anza was thoughtful. A proud man, he did not like to be wrong. Born and reared in the parched desert state of

Sonora, he knew little about rivers. Father Font, on the other hand, came from Spain and was a scholar. "Yes, you are right," Anza agreed abruptly. "I was about to come to the same conclusion. It is a lake."

Thus Anza, who had contributed so much to California, failed to recognize the Sacramento River whose tributaries were to be the trails to California's gold. But Juan Bautista de Anza can hardly be blamed for the fact that the Spaniards, the great treasure seekers of the Americas, did not find California's gold. A few years later when his mistake was discovered and the Spaniards learned of the existence of the Sacramento and San Joaquin rivers, little interest was shown in exploring or settling along them.

Unlike the Americans who opened frontiers by following waterways, the Spanish colonists preferred to keep their towns and ranches close to the coast.

Life in the Spanish period that followed the arrival of Anza's settlers was good. More colonists came. Under Father Serra and his successor, Father Lausen, a chain of twenty-one missions was eventually established along the coast. With hundreds, often thousands, of Indians working in their fields and industries, the missions grew fabulously wealthy. Though the missions were gradually secularized and their lands divided following Mexico's independence from Spain in 1822, the church buildings remain today: some in active use, others as carefully preserved historical ruins.

The Spanish ranchos grew rich also with their great cattle herds. There was little need for gold or coin in California, for with hides and tallow the settlers traded for what they needed. It was a pastoral life, a happy sometimes even lazy life, marked by roundups, fandangos, fiestas and much visiting between friendly neighbors. Spain's intention had been to make these people self-sufficient and that they became, so self-sufficient that even their ties with their motherland grew slim; and content with their isolation, they showed little interest in the outside world.

III

Enter the Yankees

If the settlers of California showed little interest in the outside world, by 1800 the rest of the world was becoming increasingly aware of them. By now two British explorers had visited the Pacific Coast. Captain James Cook (1776–1779) and George Vancouver (1791–1794), reinforcing Drake's earlier claims for British rights; the Russian American Fur Company was firmly entrenched at Kodiak Island and Sitka; and the first American fur trading ships had begun to appear in Pacific waters.

Particularly in demand were the rich sea otter pelts which brought fabulous prices in China. The American fur traders soon reached a friendly agreement with the Russians, providing their isolated settlements with supplies and carrying the Russian's furs along with their own to be sold in Canton.

Dealing with the Spaniards in California proved another matter. Spanish policy discouraged trade between its colonies and foreign vessels; however, in the miles between Madrid and the New World, orders occasionally suffered in translation, as Captain William Shaler, one of the first American fur traders, quickly discovered.

A New Englander, Shaler was both an excellent sailor and a man of reckless courage. His ship, the *Leila Byrd,* was described as being so full of leaks that it was necessary to man her pumps every fifteen minutes just to keep her afloat, but this had not stopped Shaler from coming around the Horn early in 1803, intent on engaging in the China trade.

Along the South American coast, he found the Spanish *commandantes* at several ports were quite willing to trade secretly, despite government orders. At San Blas alone he picked up enough sea otter pelts, recently brought from California, to make his voyage profitable. Learning that still more pelts were available in California, he set sail for San Diego filled with confidence.

It was only when the *Leila Byrd* was slipping into San Diego Harbor that Shaler felt his first misgivings. The harbor entrance was extremely narrow and well guarded by the eight brass cannon of a small fort at the base of the point.

Shaler's second mate, Robert Cleveland, seemed to share that same uneasiness. "I don't see why they need so many." He waved a hand toward the black maws of the guns. "They could hit the deck of a ship with a musket from there."

Noticing that neither the cannon nor the small fort seemed to be in the best state of repair, Shaler shook off some of his apprehension. "We have nothing to fear. If they have furs, they'll be as anxious to trade as the others."

At first it appeared that he was right, for the *Leila Byrd* had barely dropped anchor when a boat pulled out from shore carrying Manuel Rodriguez, the *commandante* of the presidio.

Once the *commandante* came up their rope ladder, it was obvious the visit was not a friendly one. Inquiring curtly if they needed water or supplies, he explained these would be provided them out of human decency; however, no one was to go ashore, and he was leaving an armed guard on board to make certain there was no attempt to trade.

There was little Shaler could do to protest. Once the longboat had pulled away, the four Spanish soldiers proved friendlier than their *commandante*. From the sergeant in charge, Shaler learned that just a few days ahead of them another American vessel, the *Alexander*, had visited the harbor where its master secretly had begun buying otter skins. Learning what was happening, Rodriguez had boarded the vessel and seized the furs as well as most of the cargo, leaving the Americans lucky to escape with their ship.

Exchanging helpless looks, Shaler and his men began preparations to sail, but the hints dropped by the soldiers that the local citizens were anxious to deal with them was more of a temptation than they could resist. It was decided to send two boats ashore that night under cover of darkness to see if they couldn't pick up a few pelts. One boat made it back safely, but the other, carrying the first mate and two sailors, was captured by the *commandante's* soldiers. The three Americans were tied up and left with a soldier guard on the beach.

"What are we going to do, Captain?" Cleveland asked anxiously.

Shaler's face was thoughtful. He could not abandon the three men, but it was almost certain that in the morning Rodriguez would board their ship and seize their cargo including all the fine furs from San Blas. "With daylight they'll probably move them to the presidio, and we'll never be able to reach them there. If we could just free them tonight and get out of here . . ."

Cleveland's mind was already racing ahead of him. "Give me four men, Captain, and I'll bring them back."

First, the Spanish guard was disarmed and taken below deck so they could give no alarm. It was almost dawn when Cleveland with four other sailors rowed quietly ashore. Surprising the three soldiers on the beach, they freed their companions and stroked furiously back to the *Leila Byrd* where preparations were being made to set sail.

The joy of the Americans at being reunited quickly turned to consternation as the wind that had been blowing all night suddenly vanished, leaving them temporarily becalmed. By now the sun was above the hills, and it was obvious that everyone ashore could see what they were attempting. Shaler watched in vain for some sign of Rodriguez' boat. Instead, as the sun rose higher, he and his men noticed a strange bustle of activity ashore. The entire population of San Diego, by horse, *carreta* or afoot, seemed to be heading out onto the point that guarded the bay.

The reason for the activity was soon obvious. There was no reason for Rodriguez to come out in his boat. He was going to sink the *Leila Byrd* with his cannon at the harbor entrance as she tried to escape, while the entire town turned out to watch with all the enthusiasm and gaiety of an audience attending a bullfight.

The sailors turned to Shaler with questioning eyes. The captain's mind was already made up. "Who wants to rot in a Spanish prison?" he asked. "Let's give them a run for their money, boys."

By now the breeze was freshening again. The *Leila Byrd*'s sails bulged into the wind and her anchor was drawn up. As she came about and moved slowly down the bay, the Spanish flag was hoisted above the fort and a cannon was fired without any shot. The *Leila Byrd* came on; a second cannon shot was laid ahead of her, but the ship held her course, though Shaler knew the next shot would be in earnest.

He was right. The bombardment of the nine-pounders began. Fortunately the Spaniards' gunpowder was poor and their marksmanship almost as bad, but as the *Leila Byrd* drew closer several shots tore through her sails. Shaler ordered the four soldiers brought on deck and placed in the line of fire of their comrades. By now the ship was so close that it seemed impossible that the men at the fort did not hear the yells of the prisoners. Each time there was a puff of white smoke, the frightened soldiers threw themselves flat on the deck, then scrambled back to their feet, yelling for their comrades to stop firing. Another shot ripped through the canvas. One struck below decks and sailors rushed to stuff the hole.

Opposing the fort's nine-pounders, Shaler had six small three-pounders which he ordered lined up facing the fort. Finally, they were within range to return the fire. With the first barrage from the *Leila Byrd,* the townspeople could be seen scattering wildly on the hillside. With the second broadside, the Spanish cannon ceased firing. The fort had not been hit, but apparently it had never occurred to the Spaniards that the small vessel would have the audacity to fire back and spoil their fun. Within seconds the fort appeared deserted, except for a single soldier, standing atop a wall waving his cap as the *Leila Byrd* slipped by into open water. Safely up the coast, Shaler put the four grateful prisoners ashore.

Needless to say Shaler had lost his desire to pursue any friendship with the citizens of California. Though none were quite as dramatic, similar unpleasant incidents occurred to other fur traders. For the twenty years that the fur trade flourished along the coast, the American fur vessels made little contact with the Spanish, but they carried home tales of what they had seen of the coastline.

Soon American whaling vessels were following them into Pacific waters. The whalers were often at sea for as long as three years and had to seek ports to take on supplies. Since they offered no threat to Spanish trade, the authorities relaxed their policies somewhat. San Francisco Bay became a favorite rendezvous, with as many as forty American whaling vessels laying at anchor at one time.

Meanwhile world events were shaping up to break down California's isolation even further. By 1812 American and British fur men were active at the mouth of the Columbia River. The Russians, seeking a source of supplies for their Alaskan settlements, had moved south to build Fort Ross only a short distance north of San Francisco Bay. If Spain did not protest these encroachments, it was because she could not. Her great empire was crumbling. Her South American colonies had begun their wars of independence. In 1812 Mexico joined them. Supply ships stopped coming up the coast, and for the next ten years the California colony was virtually forgotten.

Though the Californians produced the agricultural products to keep themselves alive, they had lost their source of manufactured goods and luxuries. The United States rushed to fill their need with trading ships from New England. Most historians agree that these "Boston ships" did more to win California for the United States than all the shots fired in the Mexican War. Soon more than a hundred trading vessels were working along the coast, picking up California cow hides needed in New England's booming shoe industries and bringing the Californians everything from cutlery to needles. In order to arrange transactions it was necessary for the vessels to put representatives ashore. Some intermarried into Spanish families and became permanent residents. Other adventurous American merchants began to arrive and set up independent stores in the major towns to further facilitate trade. By 1822, when Mexico won her independence from Spain, the American trade had become vital to California economy.

The first United States advance on California had come by sea from the Atlantic Coast. Not long after the Mexican flag was raised over the capital at Monterey, a second advance began overland from the western frontier. As early as 1804 Lewis and Clark had led their historic expedition to the Pacific Coast. In 1818 England and the United States agreed to a joint occupation of Oregon. As American frontiersmen and mountain men pushed farther and farther west in search of new trapping grounds it was only natural that their trails should eventually lead to California. Though the Mexican authorities had been forced to accept the Americans who arrived by sea as a necessary evil, they greeted the first overland arrivals with the same unfriendly, isolationist attitude with which their Spanish predecessors had greeted William Shaler.

In 1826, Jedediah Smith was the first to arrive overland with a party of trappers. He and his men were given a friendly greeting by the fathers at the San Gabriel Mission, but the Mexican governor turned down their request to travel north through the state to reach the Russian settlement at Fort Ross.

A year later, James Ohio Pattie and his father, Sylvester, brought the second party into California. The Patties had already survived a lifetime of adventure. They had trapped around Santa Fe, New Mexico. Later, while the elder Pattie operated some copper mines at Santa Rita for the Mexican government, James had joined in several unsuccessful trapping ventures as far west as the Colorado River. Finally in 1827 when the Mexican government canceled their mining contract, father and son headed west again with another trapping brigade. Going down the Colorado River through virtually virgin country, they took hundreds of beaver pelts without effort. It was only when they neared the Gulf of California that they discovered their error. Here, the great tidal bore that rushed up the river prevented them fom going on. Meanwhile the spring floods had closed in behind them, and they could not get their canoes back up the river.

In desperation, they buried their furs, packed what food they could on their backs and started across the arid wastes of lower California. At one time Sylvester Pattie and another man were abandoned to die, but that night the others found water and were able to go back for them. At last nearer dead than alive, they reached the little Dominican mission of Santa Catalina.

Not knowing what to do with them, the fathers at the

mission notified the governor of California, and they were escorted under guard to San Diego.

Governor Echeandia had just dealt with Jedediah Smith. Now the arrival of the Patties convinced him the entire American frontier was about to move west on him. Furthermore, he knew his home government would be displeased if he failed to act forcefully, so he ordered the entire party thrown into prison.

"On what charge?" James Pattie demanded, accustomed to American courts. "We are willing to buy passports. You have to have some charge to hold us."

"You are spies of Spain," Governor Echeandia answered with the first thought that popped into his head, and on this preposterous charge all were thrown into the presidio jail. In spite of his remonstrances, James Pattie was separated from his father.

The cell into which Pattie was thrown was eight or ten feet square with stone walls and floor and a heavy iron door. For his first meal a soldier brought him a plate of dried beans cooked in rancid tallow. When Pattie protested it was not fit to eat, the soldier threw it in his face. "It's good enough for an animal like you!" he cried.

For all his ragged appearance, Pattie was an intelligent and literate man. "If being a beast is what is required to claim this food, please consider yourself as having earned my share," he replied.

Though the captains of several American vessels intervened in the trappers' behalf, they were unable to secure their release. Already weakened by the ordeal on the desert, Sylvester Pattie failed rapidly, dying alone and untended in his cell without even his son at his side. His death brought cries of outrage from the Americans as well as many local ciitzens, who by now had become interested in the prisoners at the presidio.

After that, young Pattie received somewhat better treatment, and was allowed to leave his cell occasionally to act as interpreter for the governor. He began to suspect that the governor would like to free him but dared not for fear of losing face with the authorities in Mexico. With this in mind, Pattie told him of the rich cache of furs on the Colorado. "Let me take my men back to the Colorado for the furs, and we'll pay your government well for our freedom. You can send soldiers with us."

To his delight Governor Echeandia went for the scheme immediately. "There is no need to send soldiers into the hardships of the desert; you may go alone," he added; but he was no fool. "That is, your men may go. You will stay here as my hostage to make certain that they return."

It was not exactly as Pattie had planned, but it was the best bargain he could make. While he remained in jail, his men started for the Colorado. Reaching the river, they found the furs ruined by high water. Two took off for New Mexico, but the rest, loyal to their word, returned to San Diego where Governor Echeandia rewarded them by throwing them back into jail.

Again the trappers and the governor seemed to have reached an impasse, but help was on its way from a surprising quarter. In northern California smallpox had broken out, the epidemic advancing southward with terrifying swiftness. Among the few possessions he had carried across the desert, Pattie had a small quantity of smallpox vaccine which had been used by his father at the Santa Rita mines.

This time Pattie had no trouble securing an audience with the governor. In return for vaccinating the people of California he was promised freedom for himself and his men, plus a reward of land and cattle. From ragged prisoner he was transformed overnight to "Surgeon Extraordinary to his Excellency, the Governor."

Starting at San Diego, Pattie vaccinated 1,000 people, using first his vaccine, then fresh supplies from inoculated patients. Moving north he vaccinated 4,000 more at San Luis Rey Mission, and continuing on up the state, he inoculated some 22,000 in all, not to mention the Russians at Fort Ross, who paid him a hundred dollars for a side trip to their settlement.

Pattie had earned his freedom but he experienced difficulty in collecting payment. Eventually, he sailed for Mexico to present his claim at the capital. Meeting with the same lack of success, he returned to his birthplace in Kentucky where little is known of his later life, except that he supposedly returned to California in 1849; but in addition to the many lives he had saved, he and his father had pioneered the way for the Santa Fe Trail, the southern route over which thousands of settlers someday would come to California.

Other mountain men followed Jedediah Smith and James Ohio Pattie. Though they avoided contact with the Mexican authorities as much as possible and stuck largely to the interior, they opened new routes through the mountains. Equal in importance to these first American visitors was another arrival on the coast during this period: John Augustus Sutter, a Swiss by birth. Sutter arrived in California in 1839 by a circuitous route that included the Santa Fe Trail, Oregon, the Hawaiian Islands and Alaska. His courtly Old World manner quickly charmed the Mexican governor into giving him an extensive land grant in the Sacramento Valley where he hoped to found a Swiss colony. With a handful of white and Kanaka followers, Sutter selected the location for his outpost near the junction of the American and Sacramento rivers on the present-day site of California's capital city of Sacramento. Later, in 1841, he added to his holdings with the purchase of Fort Ross from the Russians, who with the near extinction of the sea otter had lost their interest in California. If Sutter failed to attract Swiss emigrants to his New Helvetia, men of every other nationality found work in his expanding industries. Though Sutter outwardly maintained cordial relations with the Mexican government, the heavy iron cannon he transferred from Fort Ross to his Sacramento fort served to discourage close supervision by government officials, and his outpost soon became the rallying point and goal of most of the Americans coming overland.

Just as the fur traders, whalers and merchant seamen before them had spread word of California on the Atlantic seaboard, the trappers carried back stories to the frontier settlements. Added to these oral accounts came a stream of published stories of people who had been to California. Both Shaler's and Pattie's adventures were put into print. *Two Years Before the Mast,* William Henry Dana's account of his experiences on a hide and tallow ship, became a best seller.

All came at a time when people were anxious to listen. As early as 1835, President Andrew Jackson had tried unsuccessfully to purchase the northern half of California from Mexico for half a million dollars. The United States was a young and growing nation. By 1841 the frontier had pushed to the arid western limits of the Great Plains. Beyond lay what was commonly called the Great American Desert. It was generally agreed that if expansion was to continue, the next pioneers must cross this desert to some land of promise beyond. Already the first caravans of American settlers were heading west over the Oregon Trail.

In 1841, John Bidwell and John Bartelson headed a small group that broke away from one of these Oregon-bound parties and came over the Sierra Nevadas, the first American settlers to arrive overland in California. Once the way was broken other parties followed. In the years from 1842 to 1846, nine of ten emigrants heading west still followed the safer, more established route to Oregon, but ever increasing numbers turned south to California. Sutter's Fort became the goal for most of them. Many of the younger unmarried men like John Bidwell, leader of the first overland party; James Marshall, who came south from Oregon; Pierson B. Reading, who came in 1843; and strapping Robert Semple, who crossed the mountains in 1845, found jobs with Sutter. The married men with families settled along the waterways of the Sacramento River Valley, building log cabins and clearing the land in the pioneer tradition they had learned in the States. They made little contact with their Spanish-speaking neighbors on the coast, and in their small inland settlements there was much patriotic talk about California's future destiny as a part of the United States.

On July 10, 1845, a man sat at a desk in a house in Monterey, California. Though the hot summer sun shone fiercely on the streets outside, the thick adobe walls cast a perpetual gloom over the interior of the house, so that even in midday he wrote by the light of a whale oil lamp. Thomas Oliver Larkin was a prodigious letter writer. With his voluminous correspondence to friends and newspapers in the United States, he probably had done more than any other man in publicizing California. However, the letter he wrote today was no bucolic advertisement. It was addressed to the President of the United States, and it was filled with alarm.

Thomas Larkin had arrived in California in 1832 and within a few years had become one of Monterey's leading merchants and most influential citizens. Unlike many of his fellow Americans he had not married into one of the old Californian families or sought Mexican citizenship. His wife was an American widow who had arrived in California on the same ship. Though he became an intimate friend of many of the leading Californians, Larkin left no doubt from the beginning that his loyalties remained with the United States. By 1843 when American immigration had grown to the point where such an office seemed warranted, he had been the logical choice as the first, and only, American consul to California.

Now as his pen scratched across the paper it seemed to Larkin that he had good cause for alarm. The British, with barely a handful of countrymen to protect, suddenly decided to set up consular offices of their own in California. Larkin's letter left no doubt that he believed the British consul was a secret agent, his appointment the initial step in a British plan to seize California in the event of war between the United States and Mexico.

Such a war seemed very possible. Earlier that year President James F. Polk had assumed office on an expansionist platform that promised settlement of the Oregon border and annexation of Texas; in her rapid growth the United States had run into conflict on both borders. The agreement of 1818 between the United States and Great Britain to occupy Oregon jointly for the purposes of fur trade had worked successfully as long as there were only scattered trading posts and a handful of fur men in the region; but the arrival of the American settlers had changed the situation. They could hardly be expected to live under the government of two countries, and, as a result, the two nations were beginning what would become a two-year conflict over the westward extension of the border between the United States and Canada, with both countries trying to keep as much territory as possible. Meanwhile similar but even more aggravated troubles had arisen with Mexico.

Migrating westward, American settlers had moved into Texas, considered by the Mexicans as their rightful possession for two centuries. In 1836, led by Sam Houston, the Americans had defeated the Mexican army of General Santa Anna and made Texas an independent republic. Now, their successful petition to join the United States had brought outraged cries from Mexico. Diplomatic relations between the countries had been severed, and both were moving troops into position along the disputed border.

Larkin's letter confirmed rumors that President Polk had heard from other sources. The more trouble the British could stir up for the Americans in the south, the better their chances were for a favorable settlement in the north. Furthermore, in the event of war, it was obvious that Mexico lacked the ships to protect her isolated colony, and California would fall to the first foreign power to put soldiers on her soil. Long before Larkin's letter arrived, Polk had sent an emissary to Mexico to offer to buy California for forty million dollars. Anti-American feeling ran so strong that he was not even granted an audience.

His first plan to acquire California by peaceful means having failed, Polk turned to a second, far more complicated scheme. He ordered instructions sent to both Larkin and Captain John C. Frémont, who at that moment was heading for California with a company of U.S. troops on an exploring party. The messages were too important to be trusted to ordinary means, so Lieutenant Archibald H. Gillespie, a young officer in the Marine Corps, was summoned as a special courier. "I do not need to tell you that these papers must not fall into enemy hands," the President warned.

It was late fall when Gillespie picked up his orders in Washington. By the end of year, Frémont and his overland party had reached California. Two years before, Frémont had led a similar government expedition to California. The fact that his soldiers, supposedly on a scientific mission, traveled heavily armed, including a howitzer cannon, had not endeared them to the Californians. Leaving his main party camped near the mountains, he came on to Monterey. With the assistance of Larkin, he received permission to winter in California, provided he stay inland; but when his troops appeared on the coast twenty-five miles from the capital, he was ordered out of the country. This time even

Larkin was powerless to help, and Frémont and his men began a slow retreat toward Oregon.

Not long after Frémont had started for Oregon an American vessel arrived in Monterey with a number of passengers from Hawaii. Among them was a young convalescent merchant from the East Coast, who, seeking a sea change, had traveled by ship to Vera Cruz, crossed the mainland of Mexico to Mazatlán, and caught another vessel bound for California by way of Hawaii. It was only natural he should inquire the way to Larkin's imposing adobe dwelling to seek advice in securing the necessary papers to visit in California.

"I'm an American merchant. I'd like to see the consul about my passport," he explained to the Mexican servant at the door.

Minutes later in Larkin's dimly lit study, the young merchant threw off the disguise which had carried him safely across Mexico. "Lieutenant Archibald Gillespie, special courier of the President," he introduced himself.

Knowing the risks involved, Gillespie had destroyed any condemning papers and committed his message to memory. Larkin learned of his new appointment as a secret agent. Without involving the United States government, his orders were to encourage the Californians to revolt against Mexico and set up an independent republic. It was to follow the Texas pattern except that instead of being staged by American settlers it would come from the natives themselves.

Already Larkin's mind was racing ahead to select those he could trust. There was the wealthy merchant Abel Stearns of Los Angeles, who had married into the equally wealthy Bandini family. There was cattleman William Hartnell, tied by marriage to the influential de la Guerras of Santa Barbara.

Meanwhile Gillespie carried an additional message for Frémont. Still in the disguise of a merchant he was hustled to San Francisco. Once inland, he was able to travel openly, switching mounts at American ranches along his way. After a five-hundred-mile ride, he overtook Frémont close to the Oregon border. History has never revealed Gillespie's exact message to Frémont. Some people claim Frémont acted independently, others that he acted on orders. Either way, his actions were clear enough. Wheeling around, he marched back into California, where in May he set up camp at the Marysville Buttes on the Sacramento River north of Sutter's Fort.

Frémont's dismissal from California, Gillespie's frantic ride, Frémont's abrupt return, sent a flurry of rumors sweeping the American settlements in the Sacramento Valley. Like many rumors they were completely false but nonetheless terrifying. The Mexicans were selling California to the British: Mexico had issued an order forbidding further American immigration to California. And the most frightening rumor of all—Mexican troops were marching up the Sacramento burning American farms as they came.

In Monterey, Larkin was deep in diplomatic plans to bring about the bloodless revolt his government had ordered; but on the Sacramento a handful of aroused American settlers decided to take matters into their own hands.

IV

From Onions to Nuggets

GENERAL MARIANO VALLEJO, A STOCKY, CONGENIAL man with mutton-chop side-whiskers, was the leading Mexican citizen in the north. His large home at Sonoma, north of San Francisco and toward the coast from Sutter's Fort, had been built while the Russians still occupied Fort Ross in an effort to thwart any southward expansion; but with the gradual decline of the sea otters, the Russian fur men had sold out to Sutter and left California voluntarily. Over the years, Vallejo had become a close friend of both Larkin and Sutter. It was even whispered that he secretly favored annexation to the United States. Trouble with the Americans was probably the last thing he expected.

Shortly before dawn on Sunday, July 14, 1846, the general, his family and house guests were awakened by shouting voices. Dona Francisca Benicia, the general's wife, was the first to fly to a window. She caught her breath. Thirty-three armed Americans, most of them dressed in dirty buckskins and trapper's fur hats, milled about the courtyard.

"We want Vallejo!" Someone yelled, "Send out the Mexican despot!"

Soon others took up the words. "Vallejo! Vallejo!" It became a chant. Someone fired a gun into the air; a rock rattled against the house.

Her face pale, Dona Francisca spun around. "The Americans . . . they are attacking us!" she cried. "Mariano, the back door, quickly. You must get away."

Behind her, the general struggled into his clothes. "Don't be foolish, my dear. We have nothing to fear. The Americans are our friends."

Dona Francisca returned to peek out the window. The men below did not look friendly to her. More rocks pummeled the house now, the yells grew louder. She ran into the hall arousing their other guests. Below, the men were now battering the heavy front door. Her eyes descended the stairs to the rooms below, the furniture and paintings gathered by several generations of their family. Greater than her fear for these priceless possessions, however, was her fear for her husband.

She tried to stop him on the stairs. "Mariano, I beg you. For my sake, for the children, flee while you can."

Gently pushing her aside, the general ordered her back upstairs with the other women, then strode to the door and threw it open. With his abrupt appearance there was a second of startled silence; then a babble of voice erupted. Above them could be heard the general's voice loudly demanding in Spanish what they wanted. For a second the situation took on the ridiculous aspects of a comedy. The rebel settlers had not thought to provide themselves with an interpreter, and the general could not speak English. Finally an interpreter was located in the general's own household, and he learned that his home was surrounded and he was to consider himself a prisoner of the Americans, whose aim was to liberate California from Mexico and form an independent republic.

General Vallejo offered no resistance. He suggested with what dignity he could muster that since there were women inside, the rebels send in a delegation to arrange terms instead of all storming into his house. It sounded fair to the rebels. Ezekiel Merritt, William Knight and Robert Semple were chosen to represent them.

Outside the remainder of the men waited restlessly. Minutes lengthened into an hour and still there was no word from the house. Finally in exasperation, they called a meeting. Removing Merritt from command, they chose John Grisby as their new leader and sent him inside. Again time lengthened as Grisby, too, failed to reappear. To speed him up, William Ide, a settler from the north, was sent to the door.

Inside, Ide found considerable confusion. With typical Californian hospitality, General Vallejo had brought out some of his homemade wine and fiery Mexican *aguardiente.* Taken on empty stomachs after the sleepless night and long march, the burning liquor had been too much for the delegates, who were finding it increasingly difficult to concentrate. Ide wisely refused any of Vallejo's hospitality until he had completed the negotiations and surrender.

Meanwhile the crowd, which was made up of settlers, trappers and workers from Sutter's Fort, was growing more restless.

"Hang Vallejo!" "Stand him before a firing squad!" some of the more excitable settlers began to shout as the general was escorted to the door. Pierson Reading, Sutter's chief trapper and clerk, exchanged worried glances with Robert Semple, a fellow employee. Though Vallejo represented Mexican authority in the far north, both men knew of his friendliness to the Americans. After drinking the general's wine and accepting his gracious hospitality, Semple was beginning to feel guilty about their shabby treatment.

"There's no need for violence. He's offered no resistance and agreed to our terms," Semple shouted.

"Kill him anyhow as an object lesson to the others!" one voice still persisted.

The fact that Semple was more intelligent and better educated than the average settler was often overlooked in favor of a more obvious fact. Standing a brawny six foot eight, he was known as the biggest man in California. "Anyone who harms the general will have to deal with me," he cried, catching sight of Dona Francisca's terrified face peering from the second floor. When all were silenced, there was discussion of the next move, and it was decided to send the general along with several others from his household as prisoners to Frémont's camp, while his wife and younger children would be left in their home.

The Mexican flag outside the house was hauled down, and the men raised their own flag, hastily made by one of the group. On a white background, it displayed a red star faced by a crudely drawn grizzly bear. Below was a strip of red flannel and the words "California Republic."

Things had not gone according to Larkin's instructions. Instead of the native Californians leading the revolt, the Americans, following the lead of their Texas brothers, had jumped the gun and set up an independent republic. As it turned out, it made little difference.

Unable to be of assistance while he still wore the uniform of the United States Army, Frémont resigned his commission. As civilians, he and his men joined the Bear Flaggers as they marched south toward the capital. Before they could reach Monterey to raise their flag, news arrived that the United States was at war with Mexico. Within seconds, the cause of the new republic became the cause of the Union.

A United States warship, already waiting off the coast, sailed for Monterey to raise the American flag. Back in the Army again, Frémont was promoted to major and the hard-riding Gillespie to captain in charge of the land forces in California. Most of the Bear Flaggers rushed to enlist in their California Battalion.

For some time José de Castro, commander of the Mexican military forces stationed at Monterey, and Governor Pio Pico, the civil governor who lived near Los Angeles, had been at odds. Before they could patch up their differences and rally an army, northern California had fallen. Pico delivered an impassioned plea to his people to fight, but on August 13, the American flag flew over Los Angeles and Commodore Robert Stockton of the Navy declared California free from Mexico. Sailing north, he left Captain Gillespie in charge of the occupation of Los Angeles.

Both Stockton's proclamation and the selection of Captain Gillespie to head the occupation forces were mistakes. The population of the southern part of the state was predominantly Spanish-Mexican. Just as the vast herds of cattle roaming the California hills were descendants of those early herds brought from Sonora in Anza's day, the Californians themselves were largely second and third generation descendents of the settlers who had arrived in that first decade following Anza. Their bonds with their homeland had grown thin, and few had much desire to fight for Mexico, but they were extremely proud and independent.

Gillespie, young and bristling with the self-importance of his new command, had little understanding of the Californians. Within weeks his harsh regulations, martial law, seizure of arms and rigid curfew had the Angelenos in revolt. By now their leaders, Castro and Governor Pico, had been forced into hiding, but Andres Pico, the governor's brother, and two other leading citizens, José Carrillo and José Flores, rallied the *vaqueros* of the area. Gillespie barely had time to get off a rider for help before he was surrounded and forced to surrender. With unexpected gallantry, the Californians allowed him to retreat to the harbor at San Pedro on the promise that he and his soldiers set sail and depart southern California forever.

Enraged and humiliated, Gillespie had no intentions of keeping that promise. Instead, reinforced by 350 fresh troops which had been rushed by sea under Captain William Mervine, he started back to Los Angeles.

It was one of those hot, electric, October days so common in Los Angeles, with drying winds sweeping in from the desert and the temperature soaring above a hundred degrees. For miles the thirsty soldiers trudged inland across a scorched plain, dotted here and there with a few rolling hills and covered with tall, tinder-dry mustard plants. Clouds of choking, red-brown dust clogged their throats and stung their eyes. From time to time they spotted horsemen in the distance, but they gave no signs of coming closer.

"They will not attack. They know they are outnumbered," Gillespie assured Mervine.

Already heat and thirst were proving their worst enemies. After fifteen miles the weary men were allowed to make camp for the night.

Shortly before dawn the Americans were startled from their beds as a single cannonball whistled through camp. "Attack! Attack!" someone could be heard shouting.

For a moment there was milling confusion. Mervine ordered out a detachment to reconnoiter. The men returned to report sheepishly that they could find nothing in the inky darkness. There was little sleep the rest of that night for anyone, but as the first pink sunlight crept across the mustard fields, all could see the reconnaissance party had been right. Around them in every direction stretched the same barren, dusty plain without a sign of life.

The sun barely above the horizon, the Americans resumed their march. They did not have to wait long to catch their first glimpse of the enemy. Suddenly on the crest of a low hill ahead, they saw a party of *vaqueros* with a small mounted cannon. There was a puff of smoke, and a cannonball whistled over their heads. The next shot had better aim and sent soldiers sprawling. "Take that gun. Take that gun!" Gillespie ordered a charge on the hill, but it was a futile command. Before the charging soldiers were within firing range, the horsemen lassoed the gun and galloped away with it bouncing and rocking behind them.

Soon another party of horsemen appeared drawn up on the other side of the Americans. There was a puff of smoke and it was evident that they were in possession of the cannon. Next, the cannon appeared on a hill in front again. Few of the Californians appeared to have guns, most being armed only with knives tied to long willow poles, but obviously all they needed was their cannon. A small four-pounder, it had once stood in the plaza where it served as a salute gun for visitors. When the Americans first arrived, an old woman wanting to save something for her countrymen had dragged it away and hidden it in the tules along the river. Now the Californians led by José Carrillo had lashed it to the front axle of a wagon. By lifting or lowering the wagon tongue they could change elevation, and whenever the Americans came close, a half dozen *reatas* would whistle around the gun and the laughing, shouting horsemen would gallop off to a new location.

Time after time the little cannon fired on the advancing troops. Finally the Americans were forced to turn back to the harbor, carrying their dead and wounded with them. The Californians followed, still firing the cannon until their homemade gunpowder was gone. Then dragging their gun behind them, they trotted away over the hills. The Battle of the Old Woman's Gun had been a mortifying defeat for the Americans.

Fortunately reinforcements were on the way. United States troops from the Texas border, under General Stephen Kearny, already were marching west to California. Frémont with more troops was rushing from the north. Having received premature word of California's surrender, Kearny had ordered back part of his troops. This proved another mistake. He entered California with only one hundred men and suffered heavy casualties when he was attacked by another group of mounted Californian lancers at San Pascual, northeast of San Diego. But the Californians were poorly organized, almost completely without artillery owing to lack of gunpowder, and most were armed with no more than their vicious willow lances. They were unable to hold out for any length of time. In both their victories they had failed to press their advantage. A few more skirmishes and they started drifting home to their ranches and the resistance was over.

On January 13, 1847, Frémont presided over the signing of the Cahuenga Capitulation which raised the American flag permanently over California. Andres Pico represented the Californians. Elsewhere the Mexican War continued, but in California it was over. It was a peace with honor, guaranteeing the vanquished full citizenship, their land holdings and no reprisal against their leaders. It was almost as though the Californians had fought those bloody battles of San Pascual and the Old Woman's Gun out of pride, just to show their conquerors that they could fight if they wanted to.

Apparently, they had not wanted to very badly. Within weeks, under the military rule of Governor Richard Mason, California was dropping back into its old pastoral pattern. Californians and Americans mingled once again at social gatherings in Abel Stearns' mansion in Los Angeles. Mustered-out soldiers returned to their homes in the Sacramento Valley or sought work with John Sutter.

Of equal importance to the few battles fought in California during the Mexican War was the influx of new settlers it brought to the state. In the East two groups of volunteers had been enlisted to fight in California. One from New York, led by Colonel J. D. Stevenson, arrived by sea. The Mormon Battalion, recruited from the followers Brigham Young was taking west to Salt Lake, came overland. Both arrived too late to take part in the fighting, but being composed largely of young men seeking adventure, once they were disbanded the majority chose to stay in California.

Meanwhile the usual groups of immigrant families were on their way west unaware that in the course of their long journey, California would have changed from Mexican to United States hands. Only a few days after the American flag was raised over San Francisco, another party of Mormon settlers, 250 strong and led by Elder Sam Brannan, had arrived by sea. Early in 1846 the usual spring caravan had left Missouri, heading for the Pacific Coast. As was becoming customary, the wagon train was made up of a number of individual groups who were traveling together as far as Fort Hall, where the larger section led by the famed mountain man and guide, Jim Clyman, would continue northwest to Oregon, while several smaller groups would turn southwest over the Humboldt route to California.

It had been early spring when the caravan left Independence. Now it was late July as they camped in the Wyoming hills and four men stood arguing in the flickering light of a campfire.

"You're making a big mistake. Hastings' Cutoff is still new and untested," Jim Clyman protested.

"What more do we need to know than what it shows here?" George Donner, a burly determined man, pointed to the map in his hands. "By heading straight west now and going south of the Great Salt Lake we can save four hundred miles in reaching the Humboldt River." He glanced for confirmation at the two men standing behind him, his brother, Jacob, and artistocratic-looking James Reed. Both nodded.

"But you don't have any guide," Clyman persisted.

"You heard what our scouts said. Hastings, himself, is taking a party over the cutoff just a few days ahead of us. He has promised to mark the trail," this time it was Reed who spoke.

Clyman solemnly shook hands with each of the men. "I can see that it is useless to argue. You have made up your minds. All I can say is, God keep you."

The following morning, July 20, 1846, the eighty-seven people and twenty wagons of the Donner party left the others and started west over the unknown Hastings' Cutoff. It was to be a fateful decision. Tamsen Donner summed up the feelings of all of them. "Why would Mr. Hastings recommend the cutoff in his book if it was not the best route?" she observed to her husband and five children. Tamsen Donner might be George Donner's third wife, but seldom could one find a woman more devoted to her husband. Besides, the people of the Donner party, largely midwestern farmers, had depended heavily upon Lansford Hastings' new book, *An Emigrant's Guide to Oregon and California,* in preparing the journey. In addition to the stout wagons, teams and supplies recommended by the guide book, the Donner brothers carried trinkets to trade to the Indians and ten thousand dollars sewn into a crazy quilt with which they planned to build a new home in the West. Tamsen Donner had brought several boxes of textbooks to start a school for young girls.

Yet for all their careful planning, the Donner party lacked the two most important ingredients of any wagon train—manpower and leadership. Out of eighty-seven people only twenty-eight were grown men; forty were children under fourteen years of age. Though the Donner brothers were determined, hard-working men, they were stolid farmers with no knack for leadership. James Reed, the one member of the group who possessed any attributes of leadership, was so wealthy that the others were jealous of him. In addition to his three fine wagons and herd of livestock, Reed had even brought a maid to do his family's cooking!

The Hastings' Cutoff proved too difficult for the Donner's heavy wagons. Instead of reaching Great Salt Lake in a week as they had planned, it took them a month to hoist and windlass their awkward wagons through the rugged canyons of the Wasatch Mountains. Beyond Great Salt Lake they faced the longest stretch of desert in the worst heat of late summer. In one eighty-mile stretch without water, they lost half their cattle and four of their wagons. By now they had lost so much time they could see that their supplies were not going to last them through. Charles Stanton and another man were sent ahead to California to try to bring them help. By the time they finally reached the Humboldt River and picked up the California trail, they were weeks behind their schedule, sick with exhaustion and nerves frayed thin.

James Reed quarreled with a Mr. Snyder over the brutish way he was whipping their double-harnessed teams as they strained up a sandy draw. Furious, Snyder whirled and his bullwhip grazed Mrs. Reed's cheek. Instantly the men went down fighting. When Reed rose, Snyder lay dead of a stab wound.

It did Reed no good to claim self-defense. "Hang him! Hang him!" some of the angry emigrants shouted. The Donner brothers managed to silence them and a compromise was reached. Armed with a rifle and a few provisions, Reed was banished from the wagon train.

"But that's the same as death! You can't send him off into the wilderness." Mrs. Reed's pleas went unheeded. Tearfully, she and the children kissed Reed good-bye. In the first days that followed, Mrs. Reed found signs along the trail—a burned-out campfire or the carcass of freshly killed game—that told her that her husband was still alive. But in time even these vanished.

Without Reed, the discipline disintegrated even more. Instead of working together, it became every man for himself. Three of their party were already dead. They were down to fifteen wagons. Then in October beside the Truckee River at the base of the Sierras, Stanton reached them with two Indian guides and seven mule loads of supplies sent from

Sutter's Fort over the mountains. The alders of the canyons were tinted with yellow now, and though Stanton pointed out the gray clouds hugging the peaks and urged them to get moving into the mountains, four more precious days were wasted resting by the Truckee.

Once they started the climb into the hills, there was no effort to keep together. They spread out, every family for itself, every man whipping his exhausted team in a desperate effort to get over the mountains before the coming snows, with the lumbering wagons of Jacob and George Donner bringing up the rear. It was a futile race. Each night as they made camp it was colder. Each morning brought a thicker layer of ice in their buckets. Close to the summit of the Sierras, the first snows caught them. They tried to keep going but the snows piled higher, catching the wheels of the wagons. George Donner's wagon broke an axle and tipped over on top of tiny three- and four-year-old Eliza and Georgia. With a terrified scream Tamsen began tearing at boards, canvas and piles of household goods, and miraculously, the children were dug out unhurt. Throwing what provisions they could carry into their other wagon and abandoning the rest, the family pushed on.

More snows came that night. Before the scattered groups could organize, gather firewood or protect their cattle, an eight-day blizzard caught them. When it was over, all knew that they were hopelessly trapped. Animals wandering off to die lay buried now under drifts of snow where it was impossible to recover their bodies for food.

In two separate groups they made ready to wait out the winter—part of them in three hastily erected cabins beside Donner Lake, the others six miles away at Alder Creek in two canvas and brush shelters put together by the Donner brothers.

Food soon ran out. One of the men shot a bear, but as twenty-two-foot drifts buried their shelters, even hunting became impossible. Women cooked rawhide strips and made a foul-smelling soup. They had eaten their dogs; now they pounded the bones and ate those too. One family was lucky, they owned a fur rug which they cut up and roasted piece by piece.

On December 16 a party of ten men and five women calling themselves the Forlorn Hope, outfitted with crude snowshoes fashioned from oxen yokes, set out to try and reach Sutter's Fort for help. Leading them were Stanton and two Indian guides. Six days from the lake Stanton, who had risked his life once to cross the Sierras and bring them food, went snowblind and had to be abandoned to die beside their last campfire. Over a month later, two men and five women, all that remained of the group, staggered into a ranch in the Sacramento Valley. In order to survive, they had eaten the bodies of their comrades as they died along the way.

Back on the mountain the infants, the weak and the aged were dying now. At Sutter's Fort, William Eddy, who had assumed leadership of the Forlorn Hope, was organizing a rescue party, but at Donner Lake his wife and baby were already dead. At Alder Creek, Jacob Donner was dead and George Donner lay delirious with the spreading infection of a wounded hand.

On February 19, the weakened survivors in the cabins at the lake thought they heard faint noises above them. One woman, stronger than the others, clawed her way outside to the top of the snow. She fell full length, tears freezing on her cheeks. "Are you from Heaven or have you come to save us?" she cried to the seven men coming across the snowdrifts on snow shoes.

The first rescue party found fifty-two people alive at the two camps. Seven men could not save them all. They had risked their own lives coming into the mountains on snowshoes with what provisions they could carry on their backs. Gathering those strong enough to travel, they started down the mountain, leaving what food they could spare for those who remained behind.

In all, four relief parties reached the lake that winter. When the second relief arrived, it was Mrs. Reed's turn to weep with joy. Struggling through the snow ahead of the others was James Reed, the husband she had thought lost.

For Tamsen Donner there was to be no happy reunion. She had sent her oldest children out with the first relief. With the coming of the third relief, she bundled the little ones into their warmest clothes and kissed them good-bye. Her strength had held up remarkably, and the men urged her to come with them too, but she refused to leave her husband. "We'll try to send more help," one of the men promised as he lifted Eliza in his arms.

Tamsen stood in the snow waving to her children until they disappeared; then began the long walk back to the camp at Alder Creek. When the fourth and final relief party got through to the lake, a single man remained alive at the cabins. At Alder Creek, their shouts brought no answer. Tamsen Donner's frozen body lay beside that of her husband.

Of the eighty-seven members of the Donner party who had left Independence only forty-five had reached California. Throughout California, citizens collected funds to try to give the survivors a fresh start, but as the harrowing details of their ordeal spread east, many a family changed its mind about coming west. California might be part of the Union but it still seemed very far away.

In 1842, five years before the Donners came to California and Andres Pico and John Frémont sat down to sign the capitulation at Cahuenga Pass, a small and rather insignificant event had taken place in the hills back of Los Angeles. Don Francisco Lopez, a young third-generation Californian, had gone hunting. At noon, he sat down to rest in the shade of an oak while his servant prepared lunch. Remembering that his wife had asked him to bring back a few wild onions, Don Francisco took out his hunting knife and began digging up a few that grew under the tree. Clinging to the long, threadlike roots were tiny glittering particles. "Gold! I've found gold," he shouted to his startled servant.

He had indeed found gold, enough so that the Lopez family carried on successful mining operations for a number of years. Yet the discovery caused no great interest. In 1843 Abel Stearns sent a packet of gold dust to the United States Mint at Philadelphia, the first California gold ever to be coined. In Philadelphia, it caused little comment. After all, California belonged to Mexico and it was miles away.

Now, on January 24, 1848, James Marshall had discovered gold in his millrace, quite by accident as Don Francisco Lopez had done. How things had changed in those five years between onions and nuggets! James Marshall's cry of *Gold!* would be heard around the world.

V

The Secret's Out

In spite of his occasional moodiness, James Marshall was an intelligent and practical man. Born in New Jersey in 1813, by the time he left home at the age of twenty-one he was well versed in his father's trade of wagonmaker. In those days it was a craft which insured him a job wherever he went, and he soon drifted west to Missouri where his skill was in particular demand.

Here, he too fell under the spell of the fabulous tales of California. Marshall was particularly attracted by the stories of its healthful climate. Though lithe and vigorous in appearance, he brooded a great deal about his health and had suffered from recurrent fevers since coming to Missouri.

Still, Marshall was not one to impulsively head west like many young men, lured only by a spirit of adventure. In 1844, when he finally joined an emigrant train bound for Oregon, he traveled in the paid position of wheelwright, in charge of keeping the lumbering wagons in repair on the long trek. Unfortunately, the winter snows and rains of Oregon suited his health no better than the climate of Missouri. The following spring, he joined another party heading south into California. Their destination was Sutter's Fort, and within hours after their arrival Marshall's skill had found him a job again. Later with other young Yankees who worked for Sutter, he joined Frémont's California Battalion. Mustered out of the army, he returned to Sutter to receive the offer of partnership in the mill.

Perhaps it was that cold January rain or a trace of his Yankee caution that cooled Marshall's ardor when he returned to Coloma from his trip to see Sutter. Suddenly the half-finished mill seemed a stable, secure thing contrasted to golden riches that were still little more than a dream. By the time he reached the mill site, soaked and chilled to the bone, his wild mood of elation had almost vanished. Not so that of his men when they heard of Sutter's decision that the particles were really gold. As they cheered and slapped each other's backs, Marshall cautioned them that much would depend on Sutter's coming visit. He even let them in on an innocent little plot that he had devised during the last hour of his cold ride.

It was well known that when Sutter was pleased with something he would produce a bottle of his best whisky and pass it among his workmen. "Now we want the old gentleman to be pleased with what we've found, don't we?" Marshall asked the men. "So let's all put in an equal amount of gold dust we have gathered. The first thing in the morning, Henry here will scatter it in the tailrace. When the old gentleman sees all that gold laying there, he'll be so excited there'll be drinks for everyone." In one of his phenomenal shifts of mood Marshall now seemed more concerned with a small thing like getting a free drink than golden castles in the air.

The men exchanged nods. They were not averse to a drop of Sutter's whisky, and Marshall was their boss. The gold was gathered, and on the day of Sutter's arrival, it was carefully scattered in the race.

When Sutter came, the men flocked excitedly around him, and after greeting each one personally, his Old World courtesy demanded that he also stop and speak with Mrs. Weimer before he proceeded to the mill. At last, surrounded by the jostling men he headed toward the river. As they approached the dark line of the excavated millrace, little

Mark Weimer came running across the sandbar, his eyes glowing.

If Sutter was known to reward men with whisky, he was also known to reward small boys with a coin or sweet from his pocket. "Look, Captain Sutter. Look sir, at the gold I found all by myself in the millrace!" Mark cried holding out his hat.

Marshall and the men exchanged despairing looks. Inside the small hat were all the gold chips they had so carefully planted for Sutter to find, and they dared not say a word.

Fortunately they found more gold in the millrace that day —an ounce and a half, which Sutter later had fashioned into a ring in commemoration of the event. It was enough to convince him of the authenticity of the find. Before returning home, he extracted another oath of secrecy from the men, promising them double wages and the right to hunt gold on Sundays if they would continue to work on at the mill as though nothing had happened for the next six weeks.

In spite of good intentions, it was simply too big a secret to be kept. Too many people were already involved. Sutter, in his very efforts to protect himself, was one of the first to give the secret away.

For ten years Sutter had put his heart and labor into the development of his huge outpost. He still owed heavy payments to the Russians, but gradually he was building his empire so that he could see the time ahead when he would be free of debts. In addition to his store, extensive cattle herds, wheat fields and fur trade, he had added a gristmill, distillery, tannery and blanket-weaving shops. His sympathies had been wholeheartedly with the United States during the brief war in California, and afterward many mustered-out soldiers like Marshall and those at Coloma had found jobs with him. He was astute enough to realize the effects the gold discovery could have on his agricultural empire.

Immediately on his return to the fort, Sutter took steps to

protect his interests. Though his Mexican land grant seemed indisputably legal, like many documents of those days it was so loosely worded that he had no idea of where he stood in relation to mineral rights. As his first step, he called a meeting of the Coloma Valley Indians, arranging a three-year lease of twelve leagues of land immediately surrounding Marshall's mill. In exchange, he gave the Indians clothing, flour and trinkets from his store.

Next, Sutter composed a letter to Colonel Mason, the United States military governor at Monterey, asking for mineral rights in the area and a hurried validation of his Mexican land grant. Though Sutter told no one at the fort of the discovery, his very flurry of unusual activity was enough to alert a few that something was afoot.

Sutter would not trust his letter to anyone at the fort, so he summoned Charles Bennett, one of the workers at the mill, to carry it for him. Yet on February 10, less than three weeks after the discovery, he wrote another letter to his old friend, General Vallejo, who by now had returned to his home at Sonoma. "I have made a discovery of a gold mine, which according to experiments we have made, is extraordinarily rich," Sutter confided on the basis of their long and close friendship.

Charles Bennett was not able to keep a secret any better than his employer. On his way south, he stopped briefly at the new town of Benecia being built by Robert Semple up the bay from San Francisco. In gratitude for saving his life during the Bear Flag Revolt, General Vallejo had given Semple a gift of land on the northeast shore of San Francisco Bay. Immediately after leaving the army, Semple had joined Walter Colton, the American-appointed mayor of Monterey in founding *The Californian,* California's first newspaper. Later when both found themselves pressed with other duties, they sold out and Semple turned his attention to developing his new property, where he had started a ferry service across the bay and laid out the lots of a new town to be called Benecia after General Vallejo's wife.

At the newly built store in Benecia, Bennett was greeted by Semple and a half dozen other loungers anxious for news of old friends up the river. Almost all knew Marshall or had heard of his partnership with Sutter in the new lumber mill. It was all Bennett could do to control himself as he answered their questions. His leather pouch containing six ounces of gold dust seemed to be burning a hole through his pocket.

Suddenly the door burst open and a local man, whom Bennett did not know, rushed into the store. "Have you heard the news?" the stranger called to the assembled men. "They've discovered coal on Mount Diablo! Can you imagine that? Coal right on our very doorstep!"

Within seconds the men left Bennett to surround the newcomer. That a mere pocket of coal could bring such attention was more than Bennett could stand. Pulling out his pouch, he flung it on the counter. "Coal!" he scoffed in a booming voice that carried around the room. "Take a look at the kind of coal we mine on the American River!"

Again in San Francisco and at Monterey, Bennett showed the gold to strangers. He and Sutter were not the only ones who had trouble keeping quiet. Little Mark Weimer, that precocious imp who seemed to have been born solely to upset plots, got into the act again.

One of Sutter's teamsters made regular trips hauling supplies between the fort and the mill site at Coloma. One morning he was sitting at the table enjoying some of Mrs. Weimer's cooking before starting home while Mark, restless from being kept indoors by cold weather, hovered nearby trying to attract his attention. Finally, Mark could contain himself no longer.

"You ought to see all the gold we have here!" he blurted.

"Gold, my eye! You wouldn't know gold if you saw it," the teamster jeered without interrupting his eating.

"We do have gold. My father had a big bag of it," Mark protested.

The teamster lowered his cup. "Aren't you pretty big to be telling such lies? If my father had ever caught me telling tales like that he would have skinned me alive."

Mark's eyes filled with tears at the rebuke. Behind him Mrs. Weimer's face already flushed from standing over the stove grew even redder. There were limits to what any one woman could endure—trying to raise two lively boys out here in a wilderness, cooking for a dozen always famished men, not to mention meals in between for every stranger who came by. Now this great hulking oaf, who already had dirtied her clean floor with his muddy boots, was calling her son names!

"Don't call my son a liar!" Mrs. Weimer cried in an outraged voice. Reaching into a cupboard she seized Peter Weimer's pouch of gold dust and threw it on the table. "Just take a look at that if you don't think we have gold."

The teamster took a long look, and when he got back to Sutter's Fort, he did not tell everyone, but confided what he had learned to a couple of close friends. The teamster was temporarily committed to Captain Sutter, but the next day his friends quietly left their jobs and took off for the American River. Later the teamster himself got hold of a little gold dust. Not wanting Sutter to know he had it, he passed it across the counter at Sam Brannan's store.

The work at Marshall's mill was moving at a slower and slower pace now as workers were seized by the gold fever. Henry Bigler, one of the younger men, had joined the Mormon Battalion hoping to find adventure in California. He had been rather disappointed when they arrived too late for the fighting. Now, the discovery of gold promised all the excitement that he had missed. Henry was a fine shot. On the excuse of hunting game for the table, he began slipping away from the mill more and more frequently. Once out of sight, he leaned his rifle against a tree, got his pan from hiding under a bush or rock and started prospecting. His little leather pouch grew heavier and heavier. It became a fortune and secret too large for such a young man to carry alone. He had no intentions of disobeying either Mr. Marshall or Captain Sutter's orders, but he wrote to three friends at Sutter's Fort, who were of his same Mormon faith, trusting them to guard the secret carefully. They did. At least, they did not shout it to the world but only confided it to other Mormon friends. More of Sutter's workers began mysteriously leaving their jobs and heading into the hills.

By now from his mysteriously dwindling work force, Sutter knew that his secret was out. Yet in a way, it still remained a secret too, for no one had given any official announcement of the gold discovery. From a secret shared by twelve men it simply had grown into one shared by a hundred. Then on March 15, *The Californian*, the newspaper formerly owned by Semple but published now by B. R. Buckelew of San Francisco, carried a small item.

> GOLD MINE FOUND: In the newly made raceway of the sawmill recently erected by Captain Sutter on the American fork, gold has been found in considerable quantities.

The item did not cause any particular sensation in San Francisco. It was tucked away at the bottom of the second page, overshadowed by the account of a local horse race described in detail above it.

In fact, in only one residence, at the corner of Stockton Street and Washington Alley, did the announcement cause real concern. Here a tall, handsome man of about thirty, with thick brown hair and carefully trimmed side-whiskers, strode up and down a small room with increasing fury.

Ann Eliza Brannan watched her husband with mounting

concern. "Sam, it isn't the first time *The Californian* has beaten you to a story. There's no reason to be so upset."

"Well, they haven't been ahead of me many times!" Sam Brannan, owner of San Francisco's other newspaper, the rival *Star,* declared hotly. "Besides, that isn't what bothers me. What upsets me is that Buckelew would print such a thing. It's irresponsible journalism, that's what it is! The whole story is a fake."

"Sam, are you really certain that the story isn't true?" Ann Eliza continued. "I've heard rumors. You must have heard them too. Just last night at the church meeting Mrs. Eager said that her brother had heard from a friend who knows one of the Bigler boys . . ."

"Damn it! That's exactly what I mean!" Brannan exploded. For a religious man he had a remarkable fondness for swear words. "Rumors! That's all they are, rumors! Do you suppose for a minute that if Buckelew had any proof he would tuck such a story away on the second page? If he really thought this discovery rumor amounted to anything, he'd have it in seventy-two-point type on the front page." He struck the newspaper with his fist.

"What do you plan to do?" his wife asked.

"I don't plan to do anything now," Brannan replied, "but I'll be going up to the new store soon and I'm sure going to look around. Just because a few men have picked up a couple of ounces of gold doesn't mean that its laying around like pebbles. When I tell my readers that gold has been found you can be sure it'll be worth mentioning. Too many people of this town rely on my word."

Sam Brannan was not making an idle boast. If Sutter was considered the most influential man in the Sacramento Valley, Brannan occupied a comparable position in the city of San Francisco, a rank all the more amazing considering that he had been in California a scant two years. However, on the day of his arrival, Brannan had the battle half-won. On that

July morning of 1846 when his ship *Brooklyn* sailed into San Francisco Bay, his 250 Mormon settlers already outnumbered the entire population of the town gathered on the docks to greet them.

Some would call Brannan a charlatan, others a saint. Any man able to persuade 250 men, women and children to leave their comfortable homes and sail around the Horn to found a new colony in a foreign land must have had the attributes of both. In the Hawaiian Islands, before coming on to California, Brannan had been warned of the imminent outbreak of war in California, so he armed his men and drilled them. When the *Brooklyn* finally hove to off the Golden Gate, Brannan ordered the women and children below decks and arranged his men to return the expected gunfire from the Mexican forces at the harbor's mouth. When they saw the United States sloop *Portsmouth* laying at anchor and the Stars and Stripes flying above the presidio, Brannan is reported to have cursed the flag roundly—not out of disloyalty, but because he had hoped to be the first to raise it above their new home.

If some of the citizens gathered on the dock were skeptical about these reported religious zealots who had come to live among them, Brannan proved a surprise. The powerful, handsome man with the booming laugh, ready handclasp and dandified clothes who strode down the gangplank looked more like a riverboat gambler than a man of the cloth. Within hours he was winning friends. Brannan's friendliness wasn't his only talent: within a few days after his arrival he had performed the first Protestant marriage ceremony in California. He unloaded a flourmill to give San Francisco its first gristmill, and a newspaper press to start its first newspaper. He organized the first public school and used his powerful oratory to raise money for the survivors of the Donner tragedy. With the arrival of Brannan and company the little village of Yerba Buena experienced such a surge of new life that in 1847 it officially changed its name to the more elegant and cosmopolitan title of San Francisco.

It was true that some of Brannan's own followers were becoming a bit disenchanted with their leader, especially when he displayed the Midas touch which someday would make him California's first millionaire. It was whispered that he had charged exorbitant fares for bringing his people to California and that the heavy tithes that he collected did not always go for the work of the Lord. When someone was so bold as to suggest that these tithes should be sent to Brigham Young, their recognized leader in Utah, Brannan offered a typical reply. "Tell Brigham Young I'll give up the money the day he sends me a receipt signed by the Lord," he snapped. It was not a remark calculated to endear him to his own people, but it tickled the funnybone of some of the other citizens, and San Francisco took him even closer to its heart.

In November of 1847, intent on finding new interests, Brannan made a journey up the Sacramento River to Sutter's Fort. In Sutter he recognized a kindred spirit, and they became friends on the spot. From Sutter, Brannan obtained permission to open a store at the fort. It was across the counter of this store that Sutter's teamster had paid for a few purchases with gold.

As days lengthened into the spring of 1848, more men disappeared quietly into the hills and more gold dust appeared in stores. Still no announcement came out in Brannan's paper. In fact, his young editor, after a personal trip to the American Fork, carefully noted that while gold had been found by a few men, it was in such small quantities as to be of no importance. Yet the rumors persisted. Sutter's work force had dwindled to such an extent that he was growing desperate. Brannan himself made a trip up the river.

On the morning of May 29, San Francisco was electrified. Sutter's private launch had just docked bringing Brannan back from Sacramento. Brannan didn't wait to get out an edition of his paper. His news was too great. He strode down Montgomery Street unmindful of the mud that spattered his fine clothes with every giant stride. His beaver hat was askew; his dark eyes wild. In one hand he held aloft a quinine bottle filled solid with gold dust.

"Gold! Gold!" he cried for the world to hear.

Startled citizens raced from doorways to swarm in the street behind him. "Gold! Gold from the American River!" Brannan shouted.

Brannan had no brief for secrets. There was a fortune waiting in the stream beds, the rocks, the very dirt of the California mountains. He was issuing a challenge to the world. The great gold rush had officially begun. Come and get it!

VI

Race to the Hills

"THE WHOLE COUNTRY, FROM SAN FRANCISCO TO Los Angeles and from the seashore to the base of the Sierra Nevada, resounds with the sordid cry of 'Gold! Gold! Gold!'" declared *The Californian* a few days after Brannan's announcement. Workers laid down their tools, shopkeepers bolted their doors, crews deserted their ships, and by the end of the week both *The Californian* and *The Star* had suspended publication as every able-bodied man took to the hills.

As the news spread throughout California, stores ran out of pans, pickaxes and shovels; farmers abandoned half-planted fields; cowboys left their herds. At San Jose the city jailor, finding himself torn between the gold fever and civic responsibility, solved the problem by unlocking the cell doors and taking his prisoners along to the gold fields with him.

Only at Monterey, among the native Californians, was there some skepticism. To check the rumors Walter Colton, the American-appointed mayor, had sent a man to the hills. When he returned with a sack full of nuggets, the local prophets, to salvage their reputations, insisted that they had foreseen the event all along. One claimed to have seen a white ram playing with an infant; another had watched an owl toll the church bells at midnight; still another had dreamed of gold consistently for many nights; but one old, diehard, Mexican patriot refused to be convinced. "Humbug!" he cried. "It is nothing but a wicked Yankee trick to make us think we are going to be better off living under their flag!"

Fortunately, few were this stubborn. For the length of the state, native-born Californians and Americans alike joined the stampede to Coloma. Because of the distance involved and the time that it took for news to travel east, throughout 1848 the gold rush was confined largely to the Californians and the first arrivals from Oregon and Mexico. Many of these men were friends and neighbors, and there was little lawlessness. Few of these early fortune hunters bothered to stake claims but merely wandered along the streams panning or picking up gold wherever they saw it. What these men found was largely the loose gold, the cream of the rich deposits which had been washed down by erosion, accumulating in the streams for centuries. The men who followed them in 1849 would have to work harder for their fortunes; but it would be the fabulous accounts of this surface gold, the nuggets supposedly scattered around like walnuts, that would fan the gold frenzy around the world.

In the beginning Coloma was everyone's goal but soon miners spread in both directions along the river. Henry Bigler's friends made the second rich strike at Mormon Bar. John Bidwell took a look at the terrain around Marshall's mill then journeyed north to find more gold on the Feather River near his prosperous Rancho Chico. Soon miners fanned out along the Feather, the many forks of the American, and their lesser tributaries: the Yuba, Bear and Weber Creek; this area of rivers and streams that drained into the Sacramento River was called the Northern Mines.

If gold could be found throughout the Sacramento watershed, it did not take long to figure that it might also be found along the San Joaquin, California's second great river that drained the Central Valley from the south. Charles Weber, who owned a trading point, taught some Stanislaus

Indians to pan gold and sent them home to see what they could find. When one Indian returned with a nugget weighing eighty and one-half ounces, no further proof was needed. Soon gold hunters were working along the banks of the Stanislaus, Merced, Tuolumne and the other tributaries of the San Joaquin in an area named the Southern Mines. Because it was closest to their homes, it was the region favored by the Mexican gold seekers pouring north from Sonora over Anza's old trail and the Spanish-speaking citizens from the settlements in southern California, who left their imprint in the names of many of the towns: Mariposa, Hornitos, Vallecito, Sonora.

Pierson B. Reading, a handsome, erect man with a deceptively soft voice, had come to California in 1843 after a series of personal tragedies. Once a prosperous cotton broker in Vicksburg, Tennessee, he had been wiped out in a stock market panic in 1837. He had barely recovered from this blow when he was ruined again, this time by a crooked partner who left him with a $60,000 debt. At the same time his young wife died. Reeling from the double tragedy and owing more money than one man could hope to repay in a lifetime of work, Reading headed for California with the hope of starting life over again where he was not known.

At Sutter's Fort he found work like many others, becoming Sutter's chief trapper and later his clerk. On a trapping expedition in 1844, Reading visited the area around Mt. Shasta at the far northern end of the great valley. It was a lonely, rugged region miles from the last settlement and dominated by the great volcanic mountain, which rose like a towering, perpetually snow-clad Fujiyama above the surrounding hills; but once he was back in civilization, Reading rushed to Monterey where he secured a Mexican land grant in the area. He was still employed by Sutter, but he returned to his property long enough to build a house, stock the ranch with cattle and leave a servant in charge. It seemed an ill-fated move. By spring hostile Indians had burned his buildings and destroyed his herd.

By now the troubled days of 1846 had arrived. Reading took part in the Bear Flag Revolt, served in the California Battalion as a major and distinguished himself as a member of the peace commission which drew up the treaty of surrender signed at Cahuenga. However, once he was out of uniform, Reading headed straight for his ranch. This time he made friends with the Indians, built a new adobe house and optimistically ignored his past troubles by naming the spot Rancho Buenaventura—Ranch of Good Fortune. Only one thorn marred his new happiness. He was an honorable man, and back in Tennessee there were people to whom he still owed money.

Late in February of 1848, Reading visited his old friend, James Marshall. It had been just a month since the discovery of gold. The day was gray and threatening, and Marshall and Bigler were frantically trying to finish planting several acres of peas ahead of a storm, when Reading rode up.

"Go over to the camp and make yourself at home. I'll be along when we're finished," Marshall directed impatiently, then his eyes twinkled. "While you're about it, you might take a look at the richest millrace in the world."

Reading chuckled. Already he had heard rumors of the discovery; however, once he had put up his horse and paid his respects to Mrs. Weimer, he decided he would take a walk along Marshall's millrace. First, he noticed that the earth was a rather odd, reddish color, with eroded gullies and numerous exposed ledges of gravel. It was nothing at all like the banks of the Sacramento River around his Rancho Buenaventura, but on one of his exploring trips into the mountains north of his ranch he had discovered a river which he had named the Trinity because it flowed toward the coast and Trinidad Bay on the sea. As he recalled, the

Trinity River had this same red-colored soil and gravel ledges. Suddenly his face was thoughtful.

By morning a light snow had begun to fall. Marshall was annoyed because it meant that his men would be unable to work that day, but Reading, who often found it lonely at his distant ranch, seized the opportunity to sit in the warm cabin enjoying Mrs. Weimer's coffee and the conversation of the men, some of whom had served with him in the war. Once when the cabin became too warm, he stepped outside where he walked along the millrace again.

On his return, the others began to tease him. "Want us to cut you in on a share of our gold mine, Major?"

"He's out there trying to steal some of our nuggets, that's what he's doing!"

Reading grinned and shook his head. "No, I'm not going to steal your mine, boys, but you've made me so jealous I may have to go home and find one of my own."

Later that day Reading rode on to Sutter's Fort. It did not take him long to complete his business, then he was heading home. Anyone watching him as he rode through the forest might have been surprised. Gone was that air of casual disinterest; in his eyes was a strange, new gleam. Back at his Rancho Buenaventura he stopped barely long enough to change horses and throw some supplies on a pack animal; then he was heading north at a fast trot.

Long before he reached the Trinity River, Reading stopped his weary animals to make camp beside Clear Creek, twenty miles north of his ranch. While his horses rested and grazed in the tall grass nearby, Reading took a flat, tightly woven Indian basket from his pack and waded a few feet into the cold water of the stream. He scooped up a small amount of river gravel and water and sloshed it back and forth as he had seen the men demonstrate at Marshall's mill. He dipped up more water, letting the fine soil wash away while the heavier grains settled to the bottom. A tremendous pounding began in his chest as he saw the sparkling bits that began to appear in the bottom as the worthless sand was washed away. He had found gold already! Carefully, he transferred the precious dust to a small pouch then dipped his basket into the creek again.

For a while Reading continued to pan at Reading Bar on Clear Creek, but though he found gold enough to make an agreeable weight in the little pouch, this was not the place he was seeking and he continued north. Finally beside the Trinity River, where the banks were a reddish color and there was an exposed gravel sandbar almost identical with the one at Marshall's mill, Reading stopped again. Taking his Indian basket he waded into the water. The first scoop showed color. The second showed more. The third contained several pea-sized nuggets. That heavy pounding began in Reading's chest again. Remaining just long enough to determine that this strike was a rich one, he remounted and started back for his ranch as fast as he could travel.

It was June before Reading returned to the Trinity, but this time he was not alone. With him were two assistants and sixty-two Indians as well as a herd of cattle to supply their food. When they had pitched their tents beside the river, the camp resembled a small city. For six weeks everyone worked steadily and each night Reading transferred the gold dust for that day into small sturdy bags that grew in weight and number. Then one morning Reading was alerted by a shout from one of his assistants. Glancing up he saw a party of roughly dressed men approaching on horseback.

"Halloa there. You must hail from Oregon," Reading called in a friendly voice, noticing their buckskins and frontier clothes. "Dismount and rest and we'll fix you some food."

The men drew up their horses, but they did not respond to the greeting; instead several eyed the Indians suspiciously.

"Yeah, we're from Oregon," their leader finally admitted.

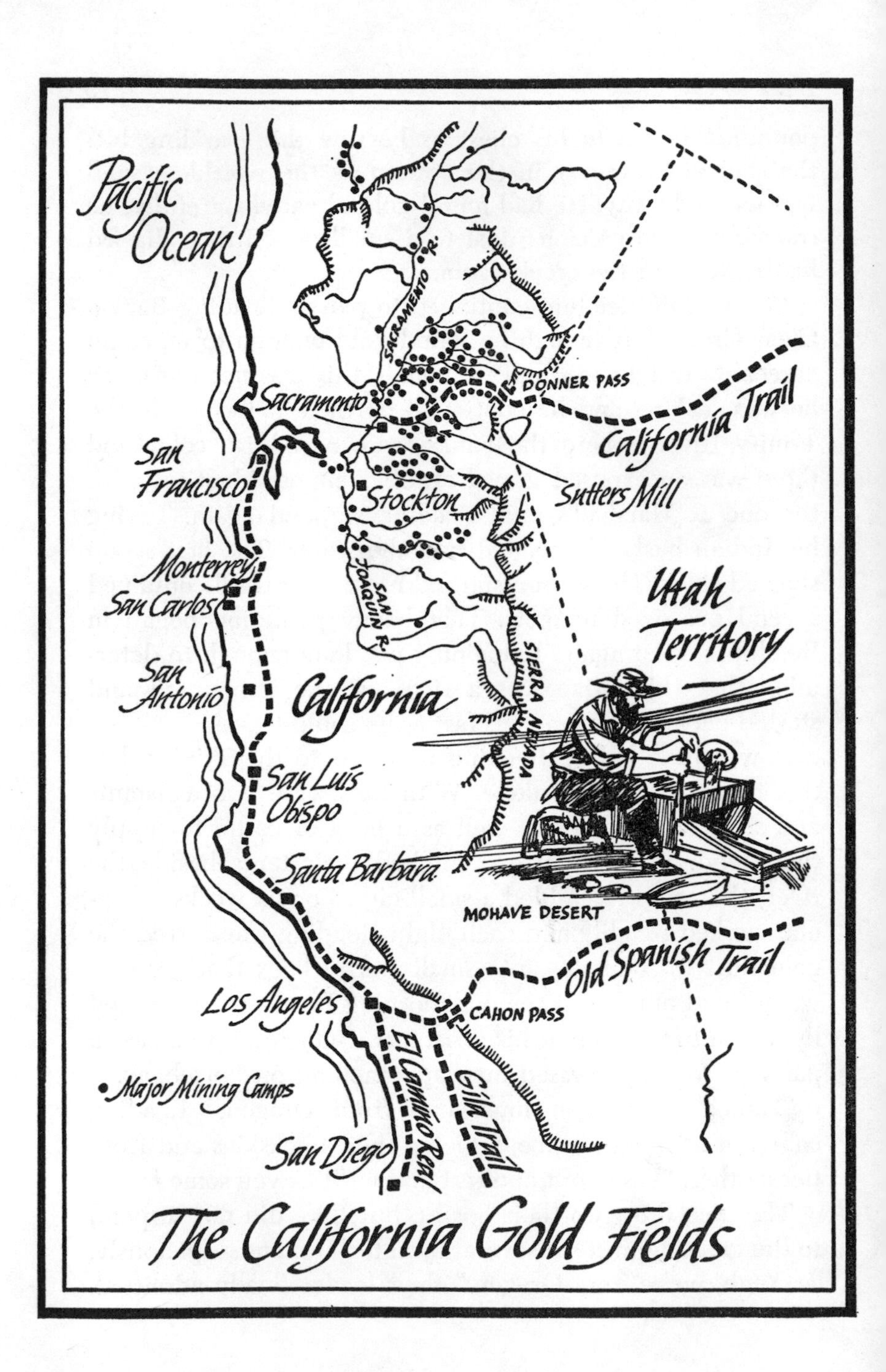
Pacific Ocean
Sacramento R.
Donner Pass
Sacramento
California Trail
San Francisco
Sutters Mill
Stockton
Monterrey
San Carlos
San Joaquin R.
Utah Territory
San Antonio
California
Sierra Nevada
San Luis Obispo
Santa Barbara
Mohave Desert
Old Spanish Trail
Los Angeles
Cahon Pass
El Camino Real
Gila Trail
• Major Mining Camps
San Diego
The California Gold Fields

"We're heading for that gold strike around Coloma. Is it true it's as rich as they say?"

"You bet, maybe even richer," Reading replied jovially, "but you don't have to go all the way to Coloma. They're finding gold along all the streams and rivers now. I'm doing all right, myself, right here."

The man's eyes narrowed and he glanced at the others. "Hear that, men? Maybe we don't need to go on. Maybe we should stop right here."

"Help yourselves, there are plenty of places along the river," Reading invited generously.

There still was no friendly response from the men. All seemed to be watching the Indians now while, out of curiosity, many of the Indians had stopped working and were watching the Oregonians in return. "We're good American citizens and Northerners. Where we come from people don't approve of slavery," the leader of the riders commented angrily.

"Slavery? What do you mean" Reading was bewildered.

"These Indians . . . they're slaves, aren't they?" the man said.

"These Indians aren't slaves!" Reading protested. "They are my friends. Some work for me on my ranch. The others are their friends and relatives. I pay them for their work, and all are free to come and go as they please."

Far from being appeased, the riders seemed to be growing angrier. "Where we come from white men do not make friends with Indians." The men were becoming menacing now, and several dropped their hands to the scabbards that carried their rifles.

"In Oregon we have only one way to deal with Indians—that is to kill them!" someone cried.

"But these are friendly Indians. They've worked for me for a long time. They've come to believe that the white man is their friend." Reading's protests did no good. He could hear angry murmurs from the riders. Many had drawn their rifles now and balanced them across their saddles in readiness. "Get those Indians out of here by nightfall or none will be left alive to leave," the leader of the riders ordered.

For a moment Reading's face was scarlet with rage; then abruptly the color faded and he merely shrugged. No one in all California doubted Pierson Reading's courage, but only moments before he had been standing in the water with his workers panning gold and he was not even wearing side arms, while all the Oregonians were heavily armed. Moreover Reading's workers had come prepared to pan gold, not fight. In all the camp, their only weapons were a couple of rifles brought along in case they wanted to add a little deer or elk meat to their diet. Less than five years ago these same Indians had burned down Reading's buildings and killed his cattle, but now they had become his friends. They worked for him and trusted him. "Break camp, prepare to leave," he called to his assistant.

Within a short time, the entire camp had been taken down, and with some of his men driving what remained of the cattle herd and the others the pack animals, Reading started away. He displayed no rancor as he raised his hand in a final friendly salute to the men waiting to usurp his place. The Oregonians would have been astounded had they known that this handsome, soft-voiced man riding away from them was completely at peace with the world, for the pack animals that his Indians drove ahead of him carried $80,000 in gold dust extracted from the Trinity River in six weeks. It was enough money to pay every penny of his debts and buy back his honor, with some left over for developing his ranch.

After a hurried trip east to pay off his obligations, Reading returned to California where he devoted the rest of his life to his ranch and never hunted gold again. In later years, he and John Bidwell shared the honors of being owners of the two greatest ranches in the north. Reading also represented his area at the state constitutional convention, was nominated as governor, served for years as Federal Indian Agent. It became a legend throughout California that, throughout his lifetime, every evening at dusk a lighted lantern was placed in the tower of his ranch to guide weary travelers to a safe night's rest at Rancho Buenaventura, whose owner had found such good fortune in life.

However, Reading's encounter with the angry Oregonians was a foretaste of what was to come. Since the mission days it had been common practice in California to employ Indian labor. Sutter employed them at his fort, Marshall used them at the mill, many of the American settlers and almost all the native Californians hired them as workers on their ranches. In 1848 many men beside Reading took their Indian workers along with them to the gold fields; but in 1849 this would end. The Yankees arriving from the east, with their bitter memories of Indian attacks on the plains, would outlaw the use of Indians in the mines; and as the newcomers swarmed over their former hunting grounds, the Indians would retreat into the mountains and former friendship would turn to hostility.

Like Reading, Bidwell and other early miners took their gold and used it to develop their California ranches or start prosperous businesses. Henry Bigler and many of the young men at Mormon Bar headed back over the Sierras before the end of the year to join Brigham Young in Utah, where their California gold stocked ranches and built attractive homes around Salt Lake City. These men, who had some other purpose in life, were the fortunate ones. For some who flocked to the hills in 1848, gold alone was the goal.

James H. Carson, a former sergeant with the New York Battalion, had reached California too late to see any fighting. By June of 1848 he was back in civilian clothes and hanging around Monterey trying to decide what to do. Some of the Spanish skepticism must have rubbed off on him, for he had no particular interest in the gold discovery; instead he was trying to make up his mind whether to return to the East or sign on a ship and see some more of the world.

One morning as he returned to his lodgings he saw a man coming toward him, unshaven, ragged and incredibly dirty. They had almost passed when Carson recognized a former friend. "Billy, what has happened to you" he gasped in alarm.

Billy's wide grin was hardly that of a man who has fallen on evil days. "I've been to the gold fields, Jim," he cried. "You'd better get up there yourself if you don't want to miss out!"

"I don't know anything about mining. I'd just wear myself out and come back with nothing," Carson scoffed.

"You know as much as I do, that's for certain. If you don't believe me, take a look," Billy lowered a sack he was carrying.

Carson's eyes widened as he saw the gold dust. "Yes sirree, stick around Monterey and be a fool if you want, but I'm going back for more," Billy said as he swaggered on.

The gold fever was a strange disease. In that fleeting instant that Carson watched Billy disappearing down the street, he was smitten. He had been thinking of signing on a ship. Why now he might buy his own fleet! Exactly one hour after the chance meeting, he had purchased a washbasin, fire shovel, blanket, rifle, some jerked beef, and was whipping an old mule, the only animal available, out of town.

Through mud, dust and thickets he ploughed up the Sacramento River Valley, reaching the gold fields at Mormon Bar, where more than fifty men were strung out along the river panning gold. Carson tied his mule to a tree, grabbed his basin and waded into the water beside them. Within no time at all, he had a dollar's worth of dust. He pushed back his hat in amazement. If he could find gold this easily here among fifty others, how much better it must be farther on!

Back on the mule again, Carson headed for Kelsey's. He found gold here too, but if the pickings were good here they must be better at Dry Diggings up the trail! A few hours of hard riding brought him to Weber's trading post. Everywhere around him men were panning successfully, but Indians from the Stanislaus were coming into the store to buy articles and paying for them with great fistfuls of gold. Carson leaned against a pine tree, feeling a little dizzy. If it was rich here, just imagine what it was like down south on the Stanislaus!

Carson did not know it yet, but he had the fever now in its most virulent form. It would never let him rest.

Two months later a strange procession wound out of Monterey, heading toward the Southern Mines. There were ninety-two men in all, representing every race, color and profession. James Carson was among them, along with George Angel, who would give his name to Angel's Camp, and the young Murphy brothers, who would be remembered by the booming mining camp of Murphys. Their organization was a loose one. For mutual protection they were riding together as far as the gold fields, but once they arrived it was to be every man for himself.

They were not the first into the area. A group of Mexicans were already panning gold beside the Stanislaus. Because this was 1848, before racial hatred had come to the mines, the Mexicans greeted them with flashing grins and held up their fat leather pouches to show that they had been successful. They had named the spot Melones because the gold they were finding came in the size and shape of melon seeds.

Heading south, Carson made his first big strike at Carson Hill. In ten days he took out one hundred eighty ounces of gold. In years to come Carson Hill would be known as one of the richest areas in California, yielding twenty-six million in gold; but Carson had the fever. Dissatisfied, he moved on, leaving only his name. He made other strikes, mined at other places where he found nothing. For him the search had become everything. Never a particularly sturdy man, he died a few years later of a rheumatic ailment, no doubt aggravated by his wanderings, rough life and long hours standing in icy mountain streams; but James Carson was only one of many who succumbed to the gold fever.

In the great gold rush of 1849 some of the gold seekers would make fortunes while others would return home penniless, but 1848 was a more generous year. Hardly a man who went into the hills that year did not come back with something for his efforts. By December there were ten thousand of them in the gold fields, and most were making anywhere from ten to fifty dollars a day. In fact, among all of those happy, successful miners of 1848, only two seemed to have found nothing but grief—the two who had started it all, John Sutter and James Marshall.

Sutter's first hint of disaster had come that morning when his first workers had slipped away to Mormon Bar. Others followed until all were gone. Leather rotted in the vats of his tannery, his looms stood idle, his wheat crop went unharvested. Younger, more enterprising merchants, such as Sam Brannan, moved their stores to the banks of the Sacramento where the miners were disembarking and took away most of his trade. For a short time Sutter made a little money selling lots in the booming new town of Sacramento, but as more miners arrived they simply squatted on his land and refused to pay him. There was no police force to drive them out. The miners killed his sheep and cattle for food, and soon they were descending on the fort itself, carrying off lumber, barrels, anything that wasn't bolted down. By the end of the year Sutter left Sacramento in despair, moving to Hock Farm, his country home near Bidwell's Rancho Chico.

Even less fortunate was James Marshall. The mill into which he had poured his labor and dreams would never saw one log. For a while he had been able to keep his workers at the mill, but soon all had gone, while daily more and more strangers poured into Coloma. They ignored his signs against trespassing, and stole his horses and cattle.

Because it was the first goal of the newcomers, Coloma attracted a rough, tough lot, and many of the miners held the California Indians in contempt. A group of toughs at Murderer's Bar fell on a camp of Indians, killed several braves and raped the squaws. In swift retaliation the few braves who had escaped killed several white men.

Marshall saw the lanterns of the angry mob as the men gathered in front of their tents. "Kill the murderers. Track them down!" angry voices shouted.

Whisky liberally doled out by the storekeepers inflamed tempers even more. The enraged miners could find no trace of the guilty savages who had vanished into the forest. Moreover, a light rain was falling, and no one really wanted to go tracking in the wet woods.

"Kill all the Indians," someone changed the cry.

Marshall saw the mob as it surged toward the mill. With him in the cabins were some of the Cullumahs who alone had remained to work for him. He gave them orders to flee, then stepped outside. "What do you want?" he demanded of the mob.

"Your Indians, we're going to hang every one," someone shouted.

"My Indians are peaceful Cullumahs. They had nothing to do with the murders," Marshall protested.

"They're redskins, ain't they?" a voice shouted.

"That's enough for us!"

"If we can't hang the Indians, then let's hang this white Indian lover instead!"

Marshall ducked back into the cabin, slammed and bolted the heavy door. While the drunken mob milled about in front, he slipped out the back way, grabbed a horse from the corral and galloped out of town.

By morning the mob had sobered, but it was several weeks before Marshall dared return. A sickening sight greeted him. In his absence, squatters had moved onto his land, set up their canvas and board shanties, and were laying out the main streets of Coloma right in front of his cabin. Seeing there was nothing left in Coloma for him, Marshall packed a few possessions on his remaining horses and left. His mood was dark and bitter; everything was gone, the mill, the gold strike, his dreams for a stable future.

Gradually as he rode, his mood changed. Some guiding spirit had led him to gold before; perhaps he would succeed again. As he rode, he had the odd feeling he was being watched, but he saw no one. At nightfall he drew up his weary animals at a quiet spot along the river and began to unpack.

Suddenly four men burst through the trees. "That's him! I told you. That's Marshall, the fellow who discovered gold!" One of them jumped up and down in his excitement.

"Found another strike, didn't you?" one of the others accused with a leer. "Thought you'd be greedy and keep it all to yourself. Well, we don't like that, mister. Get going." He gave Marshall a push.

Bewildered, Marshall stared at them. He was angry but also outnumbered.

"Get out of here, this is our strike now," the first man repeated.

Marshall rode on to make a lonely camp by the trail. The next day more people recognized him. This time it was a group of boys in their teens. They were not threatening, just noisy and exuberant as they followed him. When he set up camp, they made theirs nearby; when he waded into the river to try panning, they waded in beside him. They jostled against him, they bumped his elbows and peered over his shoulder. Finally in disgust, Marshall stomped back to his horse.

"Gee, Mr. Marshall, we didn't mean to drive you out," one lad apologized. Then his freckled face fractured in a grin. "But you shouldn't mind. Everyone knows you can find gold anywhere."

Marshall rode on, a lonely, haunted man. He pulled his battered old white sombrero low over his dark brooding eyes in the hopes no one would recognize him.

VII

Off for Californy

On February 2, 1848, nine days after James Marshall made his discovery at Coloma, President James Polk signed the Treaty of Guadalupe Hildalgo, officially ending the war with Mexico. Perhaps it was just as well that communication was slow in those days. According to the treaty, for only fifteen million dollars the United States acquired California, Texas, the major portion of Arizona and New Mexico, and Mexican claims to territory north of those states.

When the first reports of the gold discovery reached the East Coast in the late summer of 1848, they were greeted with skepticism. People had heard about California before—that land of perpetual sunshine, grizzly bears and tall tales. Fortunately official confirmation was on the way by couriers sent by both the Army and Navy, but it was not until December that President Polk in his annual message to Congress told the nation of this surprising bonus which had come with the acquisition of California: "The accounts of the abundance of gold in that territory are of such extraordinary character as would scarcely command belief . . ."

On February 28, 1849, Sam Brannan sat in the kitchen of his home in San Francisco drinking coffee. This last year, he'd had little time to spend with his family. Even now he was only home from his business interests in Sacramento for a hurried trip because he had heard there was a chance of buying another block of real estate along the waterfront. In addition to his stores at Sacramento and Mormon Bar, Brannan already owned almost one fourth of the city of Sacramento and was buying land in San Francisco as fast as he found it for sale.

"All this buying, buying!" Ann Eliza complained. "Everyone else brings home gold. All you bring home is deeds to land. Do you know how much the Bigler boys made at Mormon Bar?"

"No, I don't know," Brannan snapped, slamming down his cup, "but whatever it was, it won't be a drop beside what I'll make."

Ann Eliza tightened her lips. She and her husband did not always see eye to eye, but before she could continue the argument there was the sound of shouting voices outside. Two boys in dusty trousers raced down the street.

"A ship's coming. I think it's the new mail ship, Mr. Brannan!" the oldest boy cried as Brannan came to the door.

"She's a real steamboat . . . with a smokestack!" the other boy added. More doors flew open and men, women and children poured into the street. San Francisco was still small enough so that the arrival of any vessel was an event; but if the boys were right, this would be the *California,* the new steamer which was to start their first mail service with the East, and for some, the first steam-driven vessel they had ever seen.

Brannan raced to the waterfront along with most of the other male citizens. The boys who had spread the news already had commandeered a rowboat and were stroking eagerly out into the bay. The ship which had been visible from the top of Alta Loma, the highest hill, as she came through the Golden Gate, was hidden now by the curve of the land; but apparently the three warships anchored out in the harbor had sighted her, for they had begun a booming salute.

Unable to curb his impatience, Brannan leaped into a skiff

tied to the wharf and motioned to several friends to join him. Within seconds a flotilla of small boats containing every able-bodied man in town was heading out into the bay. Then as the *California* came around the point, laying down a fog-bank of smoke and trailing banners and bunting in honor of this inaugural run, a cheer went up from the men in the boats.

To their astonishment an even more resounding cheer came back at them. Brannan stared open-mouthed. He had never seen so many passengers crowded onto a single ship. Hundreds of shouting, yelling men jammed the decks, most of them dressed in flannel shirts, heavy boots and white straw Panama hats.

"Is it true? Is it true?" they shouted as the rowboats came alongside.

"Is what true?" Brannan called back.

"Do you really have gold out here?" One passenger's voice carried above the others.

"Gold?" Brannan bellowed, standing up and waving his arms. "Everyone in California has GOLD!"

"Hear that?" the excited passenger turned to his companions. Another wild cheer almost drowned out the boom of the cannon. The first Forty-niners had arrived!

With the acquisition of California, the need for regular mail service with the West Coast had been evident, and in the spring of 1848, William H. Aspinwall's newly organized Pacific Mail Steamship Company had begun construction of three sidewheel steamers to carry the mail between New York and Chagres, Panama, on the eastern coast and Panama City and Astoria, Oregon, on the Pacific side. In October the first vessel, the *California* had sailed from New York on her maiden voyage around Cape Horn to start the service. Since the gold fever had not yet ignited the East, she had sailed with only a modest passenger list; but while she had been making her way along the coast of South America,

President Polk had delivered his historic message. By the hundreds, miners had set sail for the Isthmus of Panama in the hopes of catching the *California* on her way up the Pacific side. When the startled captain put into Panama City he found the docks jammed with shouting, elbowing, gold-mad men. He could not possibly take them all, but he had done his best, cramming three hundred sixty-five into accommodations originally designed for one hundred, with some paying as much as one thousand dollars for steerage space.

That night San Francisco resounded with singing and laughter as the passengers celebrated ashore. Two nights later the city was silent again, as all had departed to the gold fields, but they were only the beginning. Already in ships battling their way down the coast of South America, in steady streams hacking their way through the jungle at Panama, thousands more were on their way.

President Polk's message had officially launched the gold rush in the East. Overnight, stories of California crowded everything else from the front pages. In the want ad columns lists of businesses for sale competed for space with lists of mining companies being formed to share traveling expenses. Those who could not leave home were offered shares in companies which would send expeditions to mine for them. Before the year was out, a lucky few who already had booked passage were on their way.

Young Johnny Nichols of Salem, Massachusetts, was one of these fortunate ones who sailed in late 1848. For his going-away party, his friends wrote a parody of Stephen Foster's popular tune "Oh, Susanna." Johnny liked it so well he sang it all the way to the docks. The sailors, dock workers and other gold seekers liked it so well that it swept across the United States to become the official song of the Forty-niner. Eventually it was translated into a dozen languages, and in every port in the world where the men were setting sail for the gold fields, one could hear the chorus:

Oh California,
That's the land for me:
I'm going to Sacramento
With my washbowl on my knee.

For residents of the Atlantic seaboard the logical route to California was by sea, either the long voyage around Cape Horn or the shorter trip across the Isthmus of Panama. The greatest number chose the combined land and sea route, for it was both the cheapest and swiftest. A few made the overland crossing at Nicaragua or Mexico, but the majority made the fifty-mile trip at the Isthmus of Panama, carving a path through the mosquito-infested jungle almost exactly where the Panama Canal lies today.

The experiences of Hiram Pierce, a blacksmith from Troy, New York, were typical. Like many other gold seekers, Pierce joined one of the many mining companies organized to travel together and share expenses. There was no difficulty finding a ship to carry passengers between New York and the Isthmus; and for Pierce and his party, the twenty-day voyage almost had the festive air of a pleasure cruise. It was when they found themselves on the banks of the Chagres River, their baggage piled high beside them, and surrounded by hundreds of other stranded and equally bewildered miners, that their troubles began.

Fortunately Pierce's background as a former alderman and the father of seven children had accustomed him to assuming authority. With several others of the party he secured a small launch, the *Orus,* to take them up the river, but after traveling only seventeen miles the *Orus* swung to shore.

"Why are we stopping here?" Pierce demanded. "We paid you to take us all the way."

The captain, who had been able to speak fairly good English previously, suddenly seemed to have lost command of the language. Finally he made himself clear. He had taken them all the way—all the way his launch could go. From here on the river became too shallow for the *Orus;* however, he generously offered to make arrangements for them to continue by flat-bottomed native canoe, after collecting a fee of ten dollars for each boatman. As they continued up the narrowing river in the canoes the jungle seemed to crowd closer around them. That night they made camp by the river. The following evening when they reached Gorgona at the end of the river, the boatmen watched the passengers jump ashore, then leaned sullenly on their long poles.

"Well, hurry and unload," Pierce said.

"Not paid to unload, just paid to pole boats," the spokesman of the boatmen replied.

"We paid you ten dollars, that should be enough to unload our baggage too," Pierce insisted.

The natives exchanged glowering looks. "Six dollars, that's all you paid. Six dollars, that is always the price." It did not take Pierce long to realize that the captain of the *Orus* had pocketed the extra four dollars. This made the second time they had paid for the trip up the river without getting the job done. Pierce had an ancient pistol in his luggage. It had no bullets, but when he jerked it out, the natives suddenly decided that the six dollars had included unloading too.

Three days were spent in Gorgona bargaining for the next stage of their journey. Finally for two hundred fifty dollars they secured pack animals to carry their luggage and three mules for those in their party who were unable to go afoot. The others had to walk. Two days over the rough trail finally brought them to the Pacific. Long before they reached Panama City, they could hear the ringing of the bells of the many churches, an endless, clanging, discordant sound that continued hour after hour. Two thousand miners already crowded every inch of the city, and Pierce's party joined those who had set up a tent village outside of town. Food was scarce, Americans were dying everywhere of yellow fever and Asiatic cholera, and there was not a single ship in the harbor. They nursed the ill, buried the dead, used their meager savings to bargain for food and finally, after thirty-five days, secured passage on a vessel bound for San Francisco.

Even then, their troubles were not over. The ship was unbelievably filthy and so crowded that men slept in the lifeboats and ate their skimpy rations standing up. Two weeks out, the ship almost foundered in a terrible storm as the crew battened down the hatches, imprisoning the hundreds of passengers helplessly below decks while they battled to keep the buffeted vessel afloat. It was two months after leaving Panama before the ship dropped anchor in San Francisco Bay. No military salute or crowd of townspeople greeted its arrival. By now one hundred and seventy-five vessels lay in the harbor, and the citizens couldn't care less about another arrival.

Thousands had reached San Francisco ahead of Pierce, and thousands more were on their way, but their experiences were essentially the same, as they bargained with wily natives, suffered from insect bites and fever and jammed up by the thousands in Panama City waiting for ships. By the end of the year Aspinwall and his partners, John L. Stephens and Henry Chauncey, had plans under way for the construction of the Panama Railway, but the tremendous undertaking would not be completed until 1855. Flat-bottomed canoes, ridge-back Spanish mules or their own two feet remained the answer to that fifty-mile crossing for the men of 1849.

While thousands of miners made the crossing at the Isthmus, almost all the foodstuffs, supplies and equipment for the West Coast came by sailing ship on the longer voyage around Cape Horn, and many gold seekers also chose this route. Because it was the route favored by the wealthy, the professional men and gamblers, and because the passengers often arrived with muscles so softened by physical inactivity that they were unfit for the hard work of the mines, it was dubbed the "gentleman's route." It was not without its perils, requiring anywhere from five to nine months with tedium and boredom added to seasickness, scurvy and constant danger from storms.

Mark Hopkins, who twenty years later would become famous as one of the builders of the transcontinental railway, was one of those who chose this route in 1849. Captain Tibbetts, the master of the *Pacific,* seemed the epitome of good will as he stood on the dock at New York extolling the virtues of his fine vessel with her roomy staterooms, comfortable bunks and unsurpassed cuisine; but once at sea, Hopkins and the eighty-seven other passengers received a rude awakening. The staterooms were crowded and vermin-infested; the so-called comfortable bunks turned out to be "standees," the name given to narrow, fold-up bunks installed one above another in order to crowd together more passengers; and the food consisted of raw mush and beans, with one daily serving of some unrecognizable variety of preserved meat which the passengers nicknamed "old junk."

At first, all were too miserable from seasickness to care about the fare, but once they got their sea legs, someone thought it time to speak up.

"Haven't you any pickles aboard to relieve our diet?" he asked.

"Yes, I have pickles," Captain Tibbetts admitted dourly, "but I'm not bringing them out until some of you start dying of scurvy and really need them." The captain turned out to be a bullying tyrant. When the men formed an orchestra and tried to dance on deck he threatened to install iron spikes in the planking to stop them. When the rations grew worse and a delegation was sent to his cabin to protest, he flew into a rage. Seizing a lantern, he waved it above his head. "One more complaint about food and I'll throw this lantern in the powder magazines and blow you all to California!" he yelled.

Fortunately at Rio de Janiero, Hopkins and a delegation from the ship managed to convince the American consul that Tibbetts should be replaced, but even with better fare and a more congenial captain the seven-month voyage was a miserable one, violent storms alternating with endless days of tedium before they finally reached San Francisco after seven months at sea.

Captain Tibbetts was no exception. Many captains advertised accommodations far better than they provided, withheld food from the passengers in the hopes of making a personal profit by selling the supplies when they reached California.

While forty thousand gold seekers came to California by sea in 1849, almost an equal number came overland, making the two-thousand-mile journey by covered wagon, horseback or their own two feet. The smallest number, somewhere around ten thousand, came by the Santa Fe Trail into southern California. The advantage of this southern route was that it was open year around, but it meant a time-consuming detour to all except those from Texas or the Deep South. For this reason the route used by the first settlers, via the Oregon Trail and the Humboldt, remained the favorite.

The method of travel and the hardships were the same as those faced by the first settlers. The danger of Indian attack was lessened, but the increased number of travelers created new problems. Wagons jammed up by the hundreds at the major river crossings, waiting to make the ford. The animals of the early trains ate up the feed along the trail, leaving none for those who followed. Between Missouri and South Pass in the Rockies, cholera claimed hundreds of victims. Once beyond the Continental Divide the desert became the enemy. In some waterless stretches animals perished by the

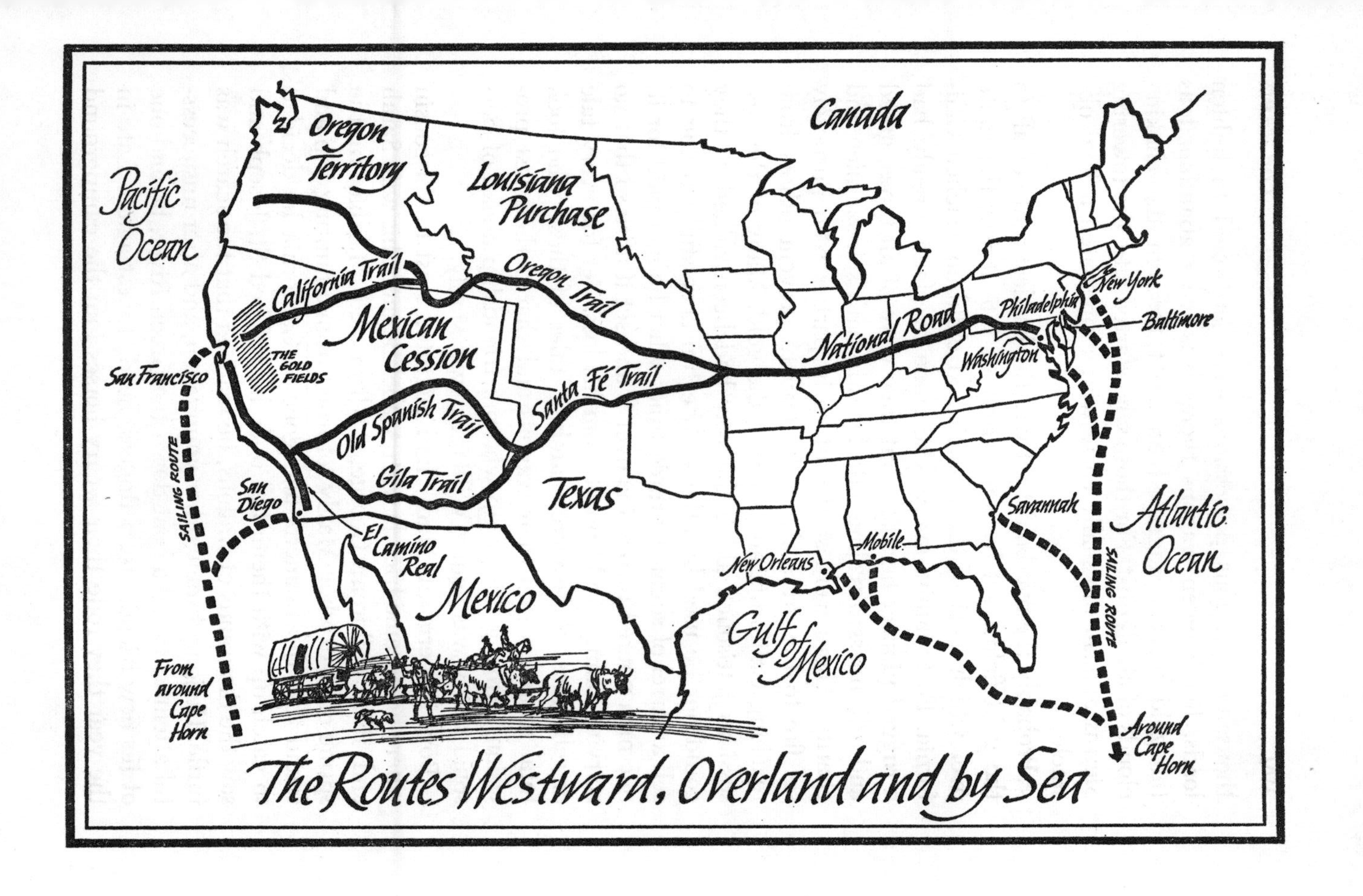

The Routes Westward, Overland and by Sea

thousands, precious possessions were jettisoned to lighten loads, finally even wagons themselves were abandoned as the gold seekers staggered on afoot through the choking clouds of alkali dust. For those who started late, the towering Sierras and an unusually early winter presented a final obstacle.

Probably the overland trail was the hardest route of all to the gold fields; yet by some irony of fate it was the route over which most of the women and children reached California. Fortunately, many who came overland already had a rugged pioneer heritage, but they were of all types, greed and selfishness traveling side by side with self-sacrifice and charity. There were stories of early parties who purposely set fire to the grass along the trail to prevent others from reaching California and sharing the gold. Many of the possessions jettisoned along the way had been ruined so they could not be used by others. After unsuccessfully trying to sell a barrel of sugar for three times what he had paid for it, one man poured turpentine over it and set it afire so that no starving family could profit from his loss. Yet for every tale of selfishness there were matching tales of those who took total strangers into their wagons and shared their last provisions. Among this group who put friendship ahead of personal safety was young William Lewis Manly.

Born in Vermont, Manly had migrated west to Wisconsin where he became friends with Asabel Bennett, his wife Sarah and their children: George, Melissa and Martha. In the spring of 1849 when Manly returned from a hunting trip and found that the Bennetts had gone to California he decided to catch up with them; but once he reached St. Joseph and saw the thousands of wagons, he realized that the search was futile. He joined some other young men, and after unsuccessful attempts to sail a boat down the Green River, he and one of his new friends, John Rogers, headed west again. Late in the year they rode their weary horses into the campground at Hobble Creek, Utah, just as an emigrant train was pulling out. As a woman leaned from the last wagon to call her children, Manly gasped. It was Sarah Bennett!

"Daddy, look who has found us!" the children cried dancing around their old friend. The Bennetts could hardly believe such a remarkable coincidence, but Asabel Bennett lost no time in persuading both Manly and Rogers to join him as drivers.

They reached Salt Lake City too late to cross the Sierras, but the Mormons were just opening a new all-year route to California by heading south to pick up the Santa Fe Trail and following it into Los Angeles. In October, the Bennetts joined a hundred wagons at Provo, Utah, where one of the Mormons, Captain Jefferson Hunt, had agreed to guide them over this new route. The new trail was rough, and by November when a party of horsemen caught up with them, many of the travelers were grumbling. The horsemen had a map which showed that by heading straight west across the desert they could reach a pass through the Southern Sierras and avoid the long trip south.

That night five hundred people gathered around the campfire. Reverend James Brier, a Methodist minister traveling with his wife and three small sons, was the most eloquent. "Why should we go five hundred miles out of our way to Los Angeles? The trail we're on now is so bad no shortcut could be worse."

Others offered similar arguments. Only Captain Hunt stubbornly insisted that he was going on to Los Angeles as long as one wagon stuck with him, but he was a gruff man of little persuasive power. "Gentlemen, all I have to say is that if you take that route you will all be landed in Hell!" was his comment.

In the morning only seven wagons continued with Captain Hunt, the rest turning west. Three days later when they found their way blocked by a steep canyon, minds quickly changed. All but twenty-seven wagons turned tail in a frantic rush to rejoin Captain Hunt. An all-male party called the Jayhawkers, Thomas Arcane and his wife and son, the Briers, the Bennetts and Manly and several other settlers, having sighted a detour around the steep canyon, decided to continue with the shortcut.

The way grew progressively worse. Finally the all-male Jayhawkers, tired of being slowed by the women and children, announced that they were pushing on alone. Leading the seven wagons with the women and children, Manly headed south, but Reverend Brier stubbornly refused to cast his lot with the family men and set out to follow the Jayhawkers alone, all unaware that their paths would cross again in the waterless, alkali wastes of Death Valley.

The Briers were the first to run into trouble when their wagons had to be abandoned in the clinging sand. Once only a sudden storm saved them from dying of thirst. Another time, Juliet Brier found pockets of dew in the rocks which she scooped out with a teaspoon for the children. By December 24, they had reached Death Valley. While Reverend Brier went ahead seeking water, Juliet followed with the cattle, carrying her four-year-old son on her back and the older boys stumbling beside her. When darkness overtook her, she knelt and felt in the sand for the tracks left by the Jayhawkers in order to stay on the trail. Finally she saw the glimmer of a campfire ahead, and her husband came up to help them on to where several stragglers from the Jayhawkers had made camp by some springs at Furnace Creek.

Though it was after midnight, they butchered one of their cows. While they sat around the fire with Reverend Brier delivering a Christmas sermon, they were startled by a "Halloa" from the darkness.

To everyone's surprise, young Manly strode into the firelight. By now his seven wagons were also approaching Death Valley and he was scouting ahead. Barely stopping to rest, he started back to his people. The next night when Manly had safely guided the seven wagons to Furnace Creek, he continued on alone after dark to make contact with the Jayhawkers who were only a short distance ahead. He found them at Salt Creek burning their wagons preparatory to climbing the rugged Panamint Mountains to the west. After learning the route they planned to follow, Manly started back to the Bennetts. On the way he met two men who were deserting his party to join the Jayhawkers. They urged him to do the same.

"Don't be a fool, man, save yourself while you can! There's no way to get the women and children out of here. Why sacrifice your life too?" one cried.

On the lonely walk back across Death Valley, Manly struggled with temptation. He was young and strong . . . the Bennetts had not waited for him in Wisconsin . . . but he could not abandon his friends.

By now the Briers had rejoined the Jayhawkers. While some of the men would die along the trail, tiny one-hundred-fifteen-pound Juliet would bring her family through, carrying her youngest child and lifting her weakened husband to his feet each morning and placing two sticks in his hands so that he could totter on. High in the Panamints, the Jayhawkers reached snow patches which furnished them life-saving water. On the other side they faced a second terrible march across the Mojave Desert, but eventually they reached safety at the San Francisquito Ranch in the mountains north of Los Angeles.

Meanwhile Manly had begun his desperate attempt to save the families. Knowing the settlers could not get their wagons over the route chosen by the Jayhawkers, he led them south, but the fourth day found them trapped in a maze of blind canyons. That night they reached a fateful decision. Instead of blundering helplessly from one canyon to another, they decided to return to the last pure water at

Bennett Wells and remain there while the two strongest men sought a way out of the valley and help. Manly and Rogers were chosen to go, the Bennetts and Arcanes giving them all of their money.

In the Panamints, Manly and Rogers picked up the trail of the Jayhawkers when they found the drying and mummified body of one of the men who had warned Manly to save himself. Crossing the mountains, they survived by sucking the tiny slivers of ice which formed on the rocks during the freezing nights; and twelve days after leaving Death Valley, they reached the cottage of a Mexican family in the hills north of Los Angeles. With the help of an American who could speak Spanish, they bought two horses, some beans, dried meat and flour. Heading back, they were able to purchase another horse and small mule.

Before they had completed three days' travel into the desert one of the horses died. In a steep canyon in the Panamints they found the way blocked by rocky falls and had to abandon the other horses, continuing on with only the mule. Already they were suffering from thirst, and after twenty-five days there seemed little chance that their friends would still be alive, yet neither suggested that they give up.

The first signs that they found in Death Valley were not promising. A man's body lay sprawled on the sand, his empty canteen beside him. It was Captain Richard Culverwell, one of those left at Bennett Wells. Finally they saw the wagons. Instead of seven, only four remained and their canvas tops had been ripped away.

"Indians!" Rogers gasped.

Manly motioned for Rogers to stay hidden while he started toward the wagons alone. He fired a rifle shot into the air.

There was a slight movement. A man crawled out from under one of the wagons. "The boys have come! The boys have come!" Bennett cried in a choking voice. Mrs. Bennett threw herself at Manly's feet hugging his legs.

Only the Bennetts and Arcanes remained at the waterhole. The story they told was a pitiful one. No sooner had Manly and Rogers gone when there was talk that since they had all the money, they would be fools to return. A family named Wade were the first to leave, followed gradually by the others. Finally even the Bennetts' and Arcanes' hopes had grown dim, and they had removed the canvas tops from their wagons to start fashioning packs to go on the oxen.

Now, they hurriedly broke camp. The children were emaciated skeletons. Two shirts were sewn together at the bottom and hung on either side of an ox called Old Crump. Tiny Martha Bennett and Charlie Arcane were hung in these pockets while Melissa and George were placed on Old Crump's back. Mrs. Bennett and Mrs. Arcane were also mounted on oxen, the remaining animals carrying their supplies. Mrs. Arcane insisted on putting on her best dress and hat, since all her other clothes had to be left behind. When one of the oxen, unaccustomed to his strange harness, became panicky his fear spread to the others. The children and Mrs. Bennett jumped to safety but Mrs. Arcane rode her bucking ox like a cowboy, her feathered hat bounding. When she was thrown but scrambled up unhurt, the others joined her in the first laughter they had known in weeks.

There was to be little laughter in the days ahead. Their greatest problem came when they reached the canyon with the falls, but the men climbed to the base, cleared away the rocks and piled great mounds of sand. Then with Manly pulling on a rope below and the others pushing above, they drove the oxen one by one over the cliff, all miraculously surviving the thirty-foot drop.

Six of these animals, slaughtered and eaten along the way, helped bring them through. On March 7, the children still hanging to Old Crump and the rest walking with ox hides bound to their lacerated feet, they reached the San Francisquito Ranch.

Most of the Jayhawkers had already gone on to the gold fields, and the Arcanes, the Bennetts and Rogers soon followed. Manly stayed in Los Angeles a few weeks working for Reverend Brier, who had gone into the hotel business; then with the little mule, he set off for the mines too. Later, he married and settled permanently in California. Historians still disagree as to whether it was Juliet Brier or William Manly who looked back from the summit of the Panamints to cry, "Good-bye, O valley of death!" giving famed Death Valley its name; but there is no doubt that their ordeal discouraged others from seeking some new middle route to California, and throughout the gold rush the Oregon-Humboldt Trail on the north and the Santa Fe Trail on the south remained the favored routes.

VIII

El Dorado

ONCE THE FORTY-NINERS REACHED CALIFORNIA, they lost no time in getting to the gold fields. If they came overland, they immediately headed for the mining camps scattered among the Sierra foothills. If they arrived by sea, they faced an additional fifty- to eighty-mile trip inland to the booming settlements of Stockton or Sacramento, the gateway cities to the Southern or Northern Mines.

By 1849 it was no longer possible for gold seekers to stroll along the stream beds picking up loose nuggets or panning where it caught their fancy as Reading and Carson had done. However, as early as 1848, miners spreading south of Coloma to Dry Diggings had discovered that gold was to be found not only along the waterways but in the dry dust of the hillsides too. Wherever one man struck gold, others followed, and camps sprang up overnight with picturesque names like Red Dog, Murderers' Bar, You-Bet, Slumgullion, Fiddletown, Yankee Jim's or Delirium Tremens. It was necessary for the newly arrived miner to stake his claim now, but usually just his pick and shovel driven upright into the earth were enough.

Where Reading had been content to use an Indian basket and Carson a washbasin, mining methods began to improve. A miner from Georgia first introduced the cradle at Coloma, and by 1849 it was already popular throughout the camps. True to its name, it roughly resembled a child's cradle and consisted of a wooden box or hollow log, open at one end and mounted on rockers. Like all the early mining devices it was based on the principle that gold was much heavier than the surrounding material in which it was found. A mixture of earth and water was poured into the top of the cradle where a perforated false bottom sorted out the coarser rocks and gravel, allowing only the finer pay dirt to sink below. Here, a series of cleats called "riffles" set in the bottom further slowed the heavier particles, catching the gold dust. The cradle, rocked back and forth by hand, could be operated by a single man. Soon, as men tried to mine more and more cubic feet of dust to show a profit, the cradle gave way to the Long Tom, a larger device which worked on the same principle with a perforated grate called a "riddle" to sort the large stones and a lower "riffle box" which caught the gold. Since the Long Tom was often twenty feet long, it required the efforts of at least two men, one to shovel in the mixture and the other to stir, and miners had to team up or work with a partner.

Because of their transitory life and the mild spring and summer climate, only a few miners built cabins of any substance, the majority living in crude tent and brush shelters. Their fare was equally primitive, for food prices were astronomical, and before the mountains became too crowded and while small game was still plentiful, a man's rifle was often his best meal ticket.

Since the miner's shelter seldom could be locked, he carried his gold dust in a poke on his person or hid it. Such careless handling of wealth was a temptation to the avaricious and the criminals who were flocking to the gold camps now, and soon men found other uses for their guns.

Like many of the Forty-niners, J. Gould Buffum was a veteran of the Mexican War, who had headed for the gold fields once he had received his discharge. In January of 1849 he was trying his luck near Coloma when a neighbor stopped by his camp.

"Did you hear the big news from over at Dry Diggings?" the neighbor asked in an excited voice.

Buffum shook his head. "What happened . . . some lucky devil stub his toe on a nugget as big as a watermelon?"

"Nothing like that," the neighbor replied. "They almost had a big robbery and killing. Last night, five men broke into the quarters of a Mexican gambler named Lopez, held a gun to his head and tried to rob him. Luckily Lopez' neighbor saw the men arrive and thought midnight was a strange hour for a visit. He aroused the rest of the camp and they caught the thieves. Tomorrow they're going to have the trial."

"The trial?" Buffum questioned. "How're they going to get a judge all the way up here from the capital that fast."

"Don't be foolish," the friend scoffed. "Governor Mason can't send a judge off to every settlement where there's been an attempted robbery. The boys are going to elect their own judge and jury. That's the only way to do it."

The following day was Sunday, the day that most of the miners took off for doing their laundry, writing home and amusing themselves, but outside of drinking and gambling, Coloma offered few amusements. Seeing that it was a sparkling, sunny, morning, Buffum decided he'd walk over to Dry Diggings to watch the trial.

The nine-mile hike was not long for a young man fresh from army service, but the way was up and down hill through the pine and oak forests, and it was late in the morning when Buffum arrived. As he neared the camp he could tell by the deserted claims and shanties along the route that everyone had already gone into town. When he finally came over the crest of a hill and saw two hundred men gathered around a huge oak tree, he realized that he had missed the trial. Stripped to the waist a man had been tied to the tree and was in the process of being flogged while the crowd shouted approval. One of the prisoners, who had already been punished, lay on the ground nearby, a raw cowhide applied to his bleeding back while the other three waited sullen-faced for their turn. Surrounded by two hundred men, the prisoners could not have possibly escaped, but as though to give the proceedings an authoritative air, a dozen miners stood in a semicircle around the tree with rifles leveled.

Slipping into the crowd, Buffum learned from a young man about his own age that the criminals, two Frenchmen and three Chilenos, had been tried earlier that morning by a judge and jury of twelve miners, found guilty and sentenced to thirty-nine lashes each.

"It's probably no more than they deserve," Buffum's confidant said. "Three of them, the two Frenchmen and the one called Manuel, tried to rob another man last fall down on the Stanislaus. I know because I was there. They weren't ever punished, just booted out of camp."

A burly, rough-looking man standing a short distance away overheard their conversation. "They ought to try them for that crime too," he voiced his opinion. "They would have killed that miner down on the Stanislaus if some of his friends hadn't driven them off, just as they were probably planning to kill Lopez."

From others standing nearby, Buffum heard angry murmurs of agreement. Being Sunday, it appeared that everyone in the diggings had taken the day off for the trial. From time to time many staggered off to a nearby saloon, the crowd becoming more drunken and unruly as the whippings proceeded. By the time all five men had received their punishment, scattered voices throughout the crowd were clamoring that three of them should be tried for the other crime.

Finally a stocky, red-shirted man, who had been the judge for the first trial, stepped forward. Calling three of the prisoners by name, he charged them with the attempted robbery and murder on the Stanislaus the previous fall. "I hereby order you to stand trial for this heinous offense," he ended rather pompously.

The order could not be carried out literally, since the prisoners were too weak from the flogging to get to their feet. While the two who were to be released were hurriedly spirited away by some companions, the three who were to stand a second trial were carried to a nearby building and laid on the floor.

Outside, the trial began immediately without them. This time no jury was selected; however, a number of witnesses were presented, and Buffum had to admit that the charges seemed well-founded. After less than thirty minutes, the judge turned to the crowd. "How do you find the defendants?" he yelled.

"Guilty!" came back a roar from almost two hundred voices.

"What punishment shall be inflicted?" the judge shouted.

For a moment the crowd seemed bewildered. The punishment could hardly be whipping, since the men already had been whipped. Then the rough-looking man, whom Buffum had noticed earlier, stepped forward. "Hang the rascals!"

"Yes! Hang them! Hang them!" drunken, angry voices took up the words like a chant.

"The unanimous verdict of this court is that the three defendants shall be hanged," the judge cried. "C'mon boys let's get on with it!"

The verdict had not been unanimous. Scattered through the crowd a few shocked faces could be seen. Buffum leaped to a nearby stump. "For God's sake, men, stop and think what you're doing. It's true these men are guilty, but only of attempted robbery. You've ordered capital punishment!"

"Maybe they didn't kill anyone but they might have if they hadn't been caught," someone cried.

"They're a bad lot; everyone knows that," another added.

"If we turn them loose, they'll probably kill someone someday."

"You can't take a man's life because of what's in the future. That's against all laws," Buffum argued. "In the name of humanity stop or you'll have this deed on your consciences the rest of your lives!" He could see the arguments were useless; already the anger of the crowd was beginning to turn against him.

"Since you like the rascals so well, maybe you'd like to swing with them," the rough-looking man suggested.

The young man who had befriended Buffum tugged at his arm frantically. "Please get down. You can't stop them. You'll only get yourself hurt too."

Buffum realized he was right. No one could change the temper of this mob. Jumping from the stump, he and his friend lost themselves among the surging men as they rushed about making preparations for the hanging.

It did not take them long. While Buffum watched grim-faced, the three victims were dragged to the back of a wagon. Ropes were thrown over the branches of the oak and attached to their necks. None could speak more than a few words of English, but no interpreter stepped forward to explain their last words. Black handkerchiefs were fastened over their eyes, and without benefit of a priest or even a prayer, the wagon was driven out from under them. When it was certain they were dead, their bodies were dumped into graves which already had been prepared.

Sickened by this sight of mob justice, Buffum returned home. He would not forget what he had seen nor would others, for the camp which had been called Dry Diggings in 1848 became known as Hangtown after that. Soon towns such as Garrote and Second Garrote boasted similar names. They were not unique. By the end of the year, there probably was not a major camp throughout the mines that did not have its "hanging tree." Lacking law officers, each camp dispensed its own justice. Lacking jails, the punishment had to be physical and administered on the spot. Flogging and ear-cropping became the standard punishment for minor offense, hanging for major crimes.

Yet for the occasional brutality of miners' justice, life in the camps had its lighter side. The average age of the Forty-niner was young, most ranging between eighteen and their early thirties, and their camps bubbled over with rowdy good spirits. In the beginning amusements were largely confined to conversation, cards or writing letters. Many miners brought musical instruments along with them; others tamed small animals for pets. Soon more sophisticated fare arrived in the form of saloons, gambling establishments and fandango halls. One form of entertainment, borrowed from the Mexicans, was the bear and bull fight. The woods abounded with bear, and promoters traveled from camp to camp presenting the fights in special wooden stockades erected for the occasion. Half of the enjoyment of these spectacles was their unpredictability. Sometimes the miners witnessed a gory massacre with both animals dying of their wounds, but almost as often the beasts refused to fight or the bear charged the audience, deciding they were better game.

One amusement that was a favorite in all the camps, because it cost nothing, was the practical joke. Usually the greenhorn was the butt of the joke as he was directed by "seasoned" miners—who themselves had been greenhorns only a few weeks before—to dig in some impossible location using some ridiculous method.

In midsummer a group of miners were at work in a ravine near Hangtown when a youth in his teens stopped to inquire politely how they were doing. It was obvious from his unstained shirt, new boots and the virgin shine on his shovel and pick that he was the rawest of newcomers.

"We're doing right fine," one of the miners drawled, winking at his companions. "Join in the bonanza if you want. Up there on the top of that hill should be a fine spot. I'd be mining up there myself right now if I wasn't already doing so good down here."

"Why, thank you. Thank you!" the boy cried, overcome by such generosity. When he had disappeared, sliding and struggling up the hill under the weight of his enormous pack, the miners leaned on their shovels and gave way to laughter. Not only did the location on the hill require an almost vertical descent to the stream for water to wash out the gold but the soil itself was as heavy as cement.

"I'll give him twenty-four hours to quit," one man said.

"Two days," another cried. "He might be the stubborn sort."

Two weeks later when the youth still appeared to be working on his forlorn and lonely hilltop, some of the men began to feel sorry for him. "He's only a lad. He probably wouldn't know gold if he saw it," one commented. Finally it was decided that the man who had started the joke should go up the hill and tell the youth the truth. If he stamped off in a rage they would consider him good riddance. If he was the type who could laugh at himself, after work that evening they would help him move his camp down to the gully and stake a claim near theirs.

Puffing and panting, the miner reached the top of the hill where his worst fears were confirmed as he saw the enormous ditch the boy had dug in the hard earth and the vertical trail he had worn down the far side of the knoll as he labored back and forth to water. The youth no longer looked like a greenhorn. His shirt was sweat-stained, his boots muddy and his skin tanned a leathery brown. He leaped forward to greet the miner like a long-lost brother, insisting that he stay and have coffee.

Feeling more ashamed by the moment, the miner finally blurted out his question. "How've you been doing?"

"Why, just like you said I would—fine." The youth led

him into his shelter where he pointed to a row of small baking powder tins lined in a cupboard. Opening the lids he showed his benefactor their contents. All were filled with gold, more gold than the jokester and all his friends combined had taken from their claims in the gully that entire season. With his first shovelful of earth from the hard soil of the hill-top, the youth had struck a ledge of almost pure gold.

Tales like those of the tenderfoot at Hangtown were what kept many discouraged men going in 1849. While the average miner labored long hours at backbreaking work to take out enough gold to little more than cover his needs, everywhere around him he heard tales of others—the man down the creek who had panned out $1500 in three days, the fellow over the hill who had dug up a nugget as big as his fist. Men who had been sensible and practical back home suddenly believed there really was a pot of gold at the end of the rainbow. If Fate could smile on one man, what was to keep her from smiling on them too? Seasoned miners as well as tenderfeet succumbed en masse to the gold fever.

The legend of El Dorado originated with the Spanish in the days of Cortez and Pizarro, when the early explorers were told tales of a mythical tribe of South American Indians who possessed so much gold that yearly they anointed a young chieftain with oil and rolled him in gold dust, which he later bathed off in a lake as an offering to the gods. The Spaniards never found this mythical tribe, but they took the words El Dorado—meaning literally "the gilded one"—back to Europe with them, and the expression spread to other countries where it became symbolic for the discovery of great riches. The Forty-niners brought the words El Dorado to the gold fields with them. Hangtown became the county seat of El Dorado County, and throughout the foothills there was hardly an area that did not boast at least one creek or claim named El Dorado; so perhaps it was not unnatural that California should also acquire a mythical Gold Lake.

In 1848 some Indians at Sutter's Fort first told of a lake high in the mountains whose shores were ringed with gold; but few knew if they had actually seen this lake or merely picked up the legend from the Spanish. Later Caleb Greenwood, an early pioneer and frontiersman, told of visiting such a lake once on a hunting trip with his halfbreed sons. Unfortunately Greenwood was an old man in his dotage, and he could not seem to remember the exact location, but the story spread so that by fall when an apparition stumbled out of the forest into the camp of two miners on the North Fork of the Yuba, the tale was widely known.

The miners had been working their cradle at the edge of the stream when they heard the faint cry. Turning they saw a man stumbling out of the forest, his body emaciated and his clothes no more than tattered shreds. "Help!" he gasped again, falling to the ground before they could reach him.

The miners carried him inside their tent and placed him on some blankets. "It's all right, friend, it's all right," one soothed while the other rushed to see if they had some whisky.

When he had taken a bit of nourishment, the stranger told an incredible tale. His name was Jim Stoddard, and weeks before he and a companion had become lost while on a hunting expedition. Wandering aimlessly through the mountains living off berries and small game, they had stumbled eventually onto a small mountain lake identified by three towering buttes. To their astonishment the lake was literally ringed with gold nuggets, and so much more lay on the floor of the lake that its waters gave off a golden sheen in the light of the sun. After stuffing their pockets with nuggets, the men had started down the mountain ahead of a storm. On their way they were attacked by Indians. Stoddard did not know what had happened to his companion. He had been shot in the foot but had managed to elude the Indians in the darkness and stagger on for days until he reached the miners' camp.

"Poor devil, I believe that story about the redskins all right; you can see the wound in his heel," one of the miners commented when Stoddard had sunk into a feverish sleep. "But all that stuff about a lake of gold—it's his fever."

The other miner nodded agreement. While his partner bathed the injured man's forehead, he picked up Stoddard's tattered coat which had fallen to the floor. "Sam! Sam, look!" he cried suddenly. From the pocket of Stoddard's coat, several glittering nuggets had fallen to the floor. The other pocket produced more.

For a moment the partners stared at each other. "It wasn't just the fever . . ." the first one began.

"Caleb Greenwood's Gold Lake! He found the Gold Lake!" the other finished jubilantly.

Stoddard was very ill, and it took some time for him to recover, enough time for his story to race from camp to camp. When he was well enough to travel again, Stoddard set out from Nevada City with twenty-five carefully selected companions to try and locate the lake. Hundreds more had clamored to go, but Stoddard had refused to take them. On the second night as they camped high in the Sierras their campfires twinkled like fallen stars in the darkness. Then one of the party who had wandered toward a bluff on the edge of the campground gave a cry. Far down in the valley below them like a reflection of their fires was another puddle of lights, still farther in the distance was another. No one needed to be told what they were; the miners who had been refused a place in the select group were following them.

The next morning they broke camp feverishly and got underway. With each passing day, as they climbed higher and higher, the way became more difficult. As Stoddard led them up one ridge then backtracked and took another, or led them several times in almost a complete circle, some of the men began to grumble that he did not know where he was going.

"You dunces!" another chided. "Can't you see he's only trying to throw off those others that are following us?"

As weeks lengthened, however, Stoddard seemed to become even more devious and uncertain. A dozen times he led them to some small mountain lake, then after looking at it motioned on to the next ridge.

"He's doing that to make the others think they've reached the lake so we'll lose them," the believers insisted; but their number was decreasing daily, and the ranks of the skeptics were growing. Finally after a month of wandering, the men had endured enough. Some claimed Stoddard was insane, the lake only a figment of his warped mind. Others said he had simply heard the legend and made up his story. Either way, all were enraged for they had given up rich claims to follow him into the wilderness. A court was held and it was decided to hang Stoddard for his deceit.

"All right, I admit I was lost for a while," Stoddard cried desperately. "I recognize those mountains up there now. If in twenty-four hours I haven't taken you to the lake, I'll help you put the noose around my neck."

His story was convincing. After a hasty meal the exhausted men crawled into their blankets. At dawn, the first one up sounded the alarm. Madman or rogue, they would never know which Stoddard was. Taking advantage of his reprieve he had ridden off and left them during the night. Aware finally that they were on a hopeless search, the men turned back.

Traveling down the mountain they met the first party that had followed them. "Where's the gold? Where's the gold?" they cried.

"There isn't any gold. There isn't any lake," the weary twenty-five replied.

The followers eyed each other. "G'won," one spoke for all.

"You found it. You're just trying to throw us off. You found the lake all right."

It did the twenty-five no good to protest. As they continued down the slope toward Nevada City, the others continued relentlessly on into the mountains, determined they were on the trail to riches. En route the returning miners met hundreds more pouring into the hills on the rush to Gold Lake. It did no good to talk to them either; they had to go on and find out for themselves. From all over California, miners abandoned producing claims to join the Gold Lake search. Newspapers warned it was a hoax; eyewitnesses told of their experiences; but it was not until fall of 1850 before the last of the gullible came out of the hills and everyone admitted he had only been following a dream.

The dream of riches was in every man's heart in those days, and none knew it better than James Marshall, hounded and hunted from camp to camp by men who were certain he could tell them the secret. At one camp a crowd of angry miners went so far as to threaten to lynch him unless he showed them gold. Only the quick action of a friend in getting him onto a horse saved his life. One day a young Australian, Edward H. Hargraves, sought Marshall out to ask where he should look for gold. Marshall in one of his now-frequent spells of ill-temper barked back at him: "Go back home to Australia and look for it there!"

One of the far-reaching results of the gold rush was that many miners, having acquired the gold fever in California in 1849, did carry it home with them, where they continued the search. Hargraves found only disappointment in California, but back home he made a tremendous discovery in western Australia that brought him a large reward from both the British and Australian governments. In his later years, Marshall liked to tell people that he was responsible for the discovery of gold in Australia too.

They might not be able to tell them where to find gold,

Gold Miners at Work

but both Marshall and Sutter had some advice for all the gold seekers that fall. They told them to get out of the mountains before the snows came. Winter came early to California in 1849. With the first snows thousands of miners poured down from the hills into Sacramento, Stockton, San Francisco and the valley towns. Others stubbornly refused to leave their rich claims and decided to stick it out in hastily thrown together cabins.

Hoping to avoid another Donner tragedy, the Army had started sending soldiers into the mountains in early fall to try and hurry the emigrant trains through the passes. As time grew short, they ordered some to abandon their wagons; and loading women and children onto a stout army mule, they hauled some bodily through the mountains, but they could not bring them all. Those caught on the other side with the passes closed above them had to turn back to Salt Lake City where the Mormons fed them that winter.

By December snows crept down from the peaks to bury cabins and isolate settlements. Some miners, underestimating the savagery of the Sierra winters, died of starvation or cold in their snow-bound camps, but with spring the hardier ones burrowed out again. As the hordes of miners came sweeping back from the cities, the hardy ones were already hard at work on their claims. The more high-spirited ones leaned on the shovels and watched the newcomers. "Dig over there, sonny," they called with a grin, as they directed the greenhorn to a worthless hard-scrabble slope or down into a gulch that was still an impassable bog.

IX

Boom Town on the Bay

FOR SAN FRANCISCO, THE THREE HUNDRED SIXTY-five miners aboard the *California* had been the beginning. As 1849 progressed and thousands of disembarking miners collided with thousands more surging back from the gold fields with money to spend, the city exploded.

Hotels crowded twenty men to one room. Prices soared. A bunk in a tent cost twenty dollars a week, a small store rented for three thousand dollars a month, the skimpiest meal started at three dollars. Such luxuries as a single sea gull egg fresh from the offshore islands, a barrel of water for bathing or a three-month-old copy of a New York newspaper brought one dollar. Lacking other facilities, gold-mad miners sent their dirty clothes all the way to China to be laundered. Small coins were virtually unknown, and the favored medium of exchange was gold dust, either weighed on scales or doled out by the pinch. Enough of this dust trickled unnoticed from the miners' clothes and pokes and was swept outside so that small boys squatted in the streets and, industriously licking their fingers or the head of a pin, picked up enough of the glittering particles to average five dollars a day.

It was a masculine society with few women seen on the bustling streets. It was a cosmopolitan society, too, with Americans, Frenchmen, Germans and Mexicans rubbing elbows with South Americans, Kanakas, Chinese and Australians, for of the forty thousand miners that poured into San Francisco in 1849, one fourth were from foreign countries.

Many of these foreign-born congregated in their own little settlements within the city. The Mexicans, Chileans, Peruvians and other Spanish-speaking peoples settled in an area of tents and flimsy shacks called Little Chile. Australia at that time was being used as a penal colony by England, and many ships from below the equator brought recently paroled convicts. Nicknamed "Sydney Ducks" by the townspeople, they gathered in a rough lawless settlement near the waterfront called Sydney Town.

Like the mushrooming mining camps in the hills, San Francisco in early 1849 found herself without organized means for maintaining law and order. Following the conquest of California, the United States occupation forces had continued the existing *alcalde*-type government, merely substituting American-appointed *alcaldes* for the former Mexican leaders. The *alcalde* was a combination mayor, sheriff and general headman of a town, a system that worked beautifully in the small towns of the Mexican era. In booming San Francisco the American *alcalde,* Thomas Leavenworth, one man without even a police force to back him up, was powerless against a rising tide of criminal activity.

The Sydney Ducks were not the only criminal element in San Francisco; the United States had contributed her share. Though many of the soldiers who had come west with Stevenson's New York Battalion in 1847 were honest, respectable men, others had been recruited from the tough Bowery street gangs of New York. Discharged from the army, most of them had joined the rush to the hills, but soon finding life in the mines too much work, they drifted back to San Francisco seeking some easier way to make a living. The lack of law enforcement presented the perfect opportunity. Banding together under an outspoken ruffian, Sam Roberts, they set up their tent headquarters at the corner of Clay and Kearny streets with a large sign reading: "Tammany Hall." Claiming to be a political organization they announced their additional intention of forming a police force to keep order in the city. For propriety's sake they chose the name Regulators; but the local citizens soon changed it to the Hounds when they saw their true intentions. During the day they paraded around town in their tattered uniforms, giving an impression of authority; but by night they looted, pillaged and assaulted at will. Their favorite victims were the weak and the foreign-born, but they soon had the entire city terrorized.

One morning in early July, Sam Brannan stood on Montgomery Street talking to several businessmen when they heard the sounds of a fife and drum. Moments later a dozen Hounds appeared around the corner marching shoulder to shoulder and grinning insolently as they forced everyone to scatter from their path. Up the street, a dry goods merchant had just arranged a display of newly arrived merchandise. Abruptly Roberts, the leader of the Hounds, gave the signal to halt. Laughing and yelling, they elbowed their way into the store. Moments later they were coming out again, several carrying new wool blankets, others with flannel shirts. One tossed his battered army cap into the gutter and slammed a white Panama hat on his head.

The storekeeper raced after them. "Thieves! Pay for those things. You have no right to take them!"

"No right!" Roberts scoffed. With one hand, he shoved the merchant roughly back against the building. "You want protection, don't you? You don't pay any taxes for a police force do you? Well, consider this your taxes."

Faced with the twelve threatening men the storekeeper retreated. It was more than Brannan could stand. Breaking away from his companions, he ran up the street. "You heard the storekeeper. Put those things back or I'll report you to the *alcalde* and have you arrested!" he shouted.

"Stay out of this. It's no business of yours," Roberts warned. From somewhere one of the ex-soldiers sprang forward and smashed his fist into Brannan's face. Before Brannan could scramble back to his feet, the Hounds were continuing up the street with their loot.

Brannan's dignity had been hurt more than his nose. "Let them go, Sam. There's no point in tangling with that outfit," one of his friends cautioned, as he helped him back to his feet.

Brannan had no intentions of letting the matter go. Barely pausing to say good-bye to his friend, he headed for Clay Street and Tom Leavenworth's office.

"I recognized most of them and I can give you their names. I want everyone arrested," he told the *alcalde*.

"Good heavens, Sam, be reasonable!" Leavenworth cried. "How can I arrest a small army when I'm only one man? Even if I was able to persuade them to submit to arrest, what would I do with them? We have no jail to hold them."

"Well, it's time someone did something!" Brannan cried.

"You figure out what we can do, and I'll be on your side," Leavenworth told him unhappily.

Though Brannan mulled the problem over in his mind those next days, he could not arrive at any solution. When he talked to some of the storekeepers and his neighbors, he got the feeling that as long as they were not being hurt personally and the tribute exacted by the Hounds was not too high, they were not ready to take action.

On Sunday, July 15, the Hounds staged a large and boisterous parade through the city, but when Brannan went to bed that night he had to admit that their principal crime had been drunkenness, and in those rowdy days that was hardly a jail offense. It was almost midnight when he was awakened by running footsteps, shouting voices.

"Sam, come out here!" Ann Eliza cried.

Pulling on his pants, Brannan followed his wife outside where he saw several terrified women with shawls over their nightgowns as they cowered on his front steps. Others milled in the street, pointing toward the northwest where a pink glow lit the sky.

"It's the Hounds. They're burning out the people of Little Chile," Ann Eliza cried.

From the frightened women on the steps, Brannan finally got the entire story. The Spanish-speaking people of Little Chile had long been a favorite target for the Hounds' abuse. At this time of year most of the men were away at the mines, so the settlement had been largely inhabited by women and children when the Hounds swooped down after dark, most of them drunk and mounted on horseback. They claimed that they came to collect some money owed by one of the residents. When he was unable to pay, they turned on the whole settlement, beating old men and children, attacking young women, entering the shanties to seize everything of value, then setting them afire. The homes of most of Brannan's neighbors sheltered other frightened refugees.

"This is enough. The Hounds must go!" Brannan bellowed.

"How can you stop them?" Ann Eliza asked.

"I don't know but tomorrow morning I intend to try," Brannan snapped.

Early the next morning Brannan began a round of the business establishments owned by the more respectable citizens. At ten o'clock someone rolled a barrel to the corner of Clay and Montgomery streets. Surrounded by the businessmen, who had accompanied him from their stores, Brannan mounted the barrel. Soon a much larger crowd had gathered.

"How long are you going to live in a city without law or order?" Brannan demanded. "How long are you going to endure these ruffians?"

There was a roar from the crowd. "How can we fight them when they're armed and organized?" someone asked.

"You're right. We can't fight them alone. But what is to keep us from organizing too?" Brannan shouted back. "I want you to go now and spread the word. At three this afternoon there will be a meeting in front of Leavenworth's office. Tell every man who is interested in law and order, who wants his wife to be able to walk the streets in safety, to be there!"

At three that afternoon one of the largest crowds ever seen in San Francisco assembled in the plaza. By climbing to the roof of the *alcalde's* office which backed against a hill, Brannan could address everyone.

First he ordered a collection taken for the destitute families of Little Chile. "The Hounds did the burning, but we share the responsibility for not stopping these ruffians sooner, so when you reach into your pockets and your pokes, let your conscience be your guide," he said.

When the collection had been taken, Brannan got down to the real business of the meeting with a lengthy tirade against the Hounds. The location he had chosen for the meeting was within sight of the Hounds' headquarters. Sneering and making sarcastic comments, a number of them mingled in the crowd. As Brannan's speech grew more violent some drew their pistols threateningly, and one of Brannan's friends whispered a warning.

With one of those dramatic gestures for which he was noted, Brannan stepped to the edge of the roof, and bared his chest. "Shoot me if you dare," he shouted, "but take a look at the honest, God-fearing citizens around you and consider how long you yourself will live after you have fired the shot."

It was the spark needed to ignite his audience. Near the front of the crowd a half-dozen men surrounded one of the Hounds, seized his gun, then manhandled him to the edge of the assembled men and sent him flying down the street. Suddenly the other Hounds began putting away their weapons and moving away.

Meanwhile the honest citizens who remained agreed that the only way to counteract the Hounds was to form a citizens' police force of their own. Calling themselves the Committee of Safety, they elected two men to assist the *alcalde* as judges, others to act as prosecutors, while the remainder were divided into groups to patrol the city streets rounding up criminals. Two hundred and thirty men armed with guns, clubs and buggy whips volunteered.

Aware that they were outnumbered, some of the Hounds fled the city, and by the following day Sam Roberts and the ringleaders of the Little Chile attack had been rounded up. Immediately a new problem presented itself.

"What are we going to do with them?" the leader of the armed patrol asked. "We haven't any jail."

Fortunately there was a warship anchored in the harbor, and the citizens made arrangements for the prisoners to be lodged temporarily aboard the USS *Warren.* Brought to a speedy trial, Roberts was found guilty of riot, robbery and assault and sentenced to ten years at hard labor. Most of his henchmen received similar sentences, but with the trials concluded, Brannan and his citizens' committee faced a new dilemma. It was one thing to lodge a criminal aboard the USS *Warren* for a few days, but they could not be kept there permanently and California lacked a prison in which they could serve their sentences. By now it was evident most of the criminal element was in full rout, so the committee took the only action possible and escorted those who had been convicted to the edge of town and banished them. Their work completed in ten days, the committee disbanded and the men returned to their businesses.

It was impossible for construction to keep pace with San Francisco's growth. As lumber ran short, many of the new buildings: hotels, stores, even one of the biggest gambling halls, the El Dorado, were constructed out of canvas. At night hundreds of lanterns shining through their flimsy canvas walls gave the city a translucent glow as though it burned with some inner fire. By late summer hundreds of vessels lay idle in the harbor, their crews having deserted to go to the gold fields. Profiting from their experience with the Hounds, the city leased the brig *Euphemia* to be used as their jail. The enterprising owner of the three-masted *Niantic* ran her ashore, piled sand around her keel to hold her upright and rented her out. Lacking warehouse space, Brannan and other merchants rented the holds of anchored vessels as storehouses.

There was no question about the city needing the cargo that Henry Meiggs brought around Cape Horn with him late that summer. A New York lumberman, Meiggs had set sail with a shipload of lumber with the idea of selling it and speculating in California real estate. When he counted the money for his cargo, he decided to stick with the lumber business for a while. However, he used his profits to buy some land out at North Beach between the city and the Golden Gate, in spite of the fact that the city seemed to be expanding in the other direction toward the mud flats to the south. The fact that people did not go for his new development right away did not bother Meiggs. Where a stream crossed his property, he built a small sawmill and began cutting lumber. Later, he built an even larger mill up the coast among the redwoods and soon had several hundred men working for him. No business enterprise seemed too big or too small for Henry Meiggs. At the same time that he built mills that employed hundreds, he also bought three washtubs, a supply of baking soda and yellow soap, and hired three husky Australian women to wash clothes in his back yard, starting San Francisco's first laundry service. Though he lacked Brannan's eloquence, Meiggs had much of his manner: the hearty handclasp, ruddy good looks and quick smile for everyone. Next to Brannan he became the most popular man in town. "Honest Harry" the people called him, and it was whispered that no man down on his luck was ever turned away from Meiggs' door.

As fall lengthened into winter and word reached the city of the plight of hundreds of wagons trapped east of the Sierras, Brannan led the fund-raising drives to send the emigrants food and clothing, but the winter of 1849 brought San Francisco her troubles too. The rains started early in October and continued endlessly day after day until they turned the city into a morass of mud. Montgomery Street, the main business thoroughfare, became an unbelievable quagmire into which horses or mules, unfortunate enough to lose their footing, were quickly sucked from sight. Load after load of brush was carted in from the hills, only to sink without trace into the ooze. Finally in desperation, the merchants started tossing in surplus supplies. Montgomery Street in 1849 boasted as part of its pavement hundreds of casks of Chilean flour and boxes of Virginia tobacco, an entire shipment of iron cookstoves, and at least one piano.

For all its rowdy masculine population, San Francisco took on a nostalgic air with the approach of Christmas. Miners who had been carousing the week before began to think suddenly of home. The stores were decorated with wreaths and red and green bunting, their windows crammed with tawdry trinkets that could be shipped to loved ones back home. Brannan had come down from his store at Sacramento to help Ann Eliza and the children prepare for Christmas. At six o'clock on the morning of December 24, they had just risen when they heard a distant sound like the clanging of bells; then there was a noisy pounding on the door.

Swinging it open, Brannan saw one of his neighbors holding a lantern. It was still dark outside, except to the east where a pink glow was spreading against the sky. Even as Brannan watched, it climbed higher.

"The whole plaza's burning. The town is on fire!" the neighbor screamed. Beyond them shadowy figures were racing down the hill. Snatching his coat, Brannan joined them. As he neared town, he passed several water wagons sunk to their axles in the mud while their drivers flayed helplessly at their straining teams.

When Brannan reached the center of town he saw that his neighbor had not been exaggerating. The fire which had started in Dennison's Exchange had already spread to the Parker House Hotel and was raging out of control.

Because of the mud that clogged the streets, it was impossible to bring up the heavy water wagons. Brannan joined the lines of men who had formed bucket brigades, but their efforts seemed useless against the flames which were fed by a strong wind from the bay. As the sun rose Brannan gazed helplessly at the sky. For weeks on end, there had been endless rain, now not even one little cloud could be seen in the sky.

Abruptly the wind changed. Flames which had destroyed all the major buildings along one side of the plaza raced back down the other side now, taking those buildings too. The tent structure of the El Dorado gambling hall ignited and went up in a gigantic pillar of flame and cascading sparks.

In midmorning, the flames shifted again. Abandoning the bucket brigade, Brannan dashed to a nearby stable. "Get a wagon up to my house quick," he ordered the owner. "If the flames reach Dupont Street start moving out the furniture." The flames shifted and reversed themselves throughout the day. In the afternoon when they started inland again, Brannan dashed home to find Ann Eliza and the drayman carrying out belongings, but once again the wind changed and the fire raced back toward the bay.

Unable to get the water wagons through the mud, the fire fighters started throwing the mud itself onto the flames. Again Brannan joined them, his good clothes splattered, then ruined; but the flames continued on through the night and into Christmas Day. Finally the leading citizens made a fateful decision. Gunpowder was brought in, and while their stricken owners looked away, a block of buildings in the path of the flames was blown to rubble. The flames roared into the ruins, then unable to find nourishment sizzled away.

The next day San Francisco started rebuilding. Henry Meiggs' sawmills worked overtime, and by New Year's Day of 1850 the scaffolding of a new business district already rose against the sky. San Francisco had to rebuild. No longer the sleepy village of eight hundred people it had been in 1848, it boasted a population of twenty-five thousand; and the rush had only begun. If eighty thousand Forty-niners had reached California in 1849, one hundred thousand were going to follow them in 1850.

X

State Without Statesmen

IN LATE AUGUST 1849, FOUR HORSEMEN RODE NORTH from Los Angeles toward the capital at Monterey. The country through which they passed was very different from that of the booming bay region to the north. Mile after mile they rode across rolling, oak-dotted hills carpeted with the velvety yellow-brown grass of late summer; the only sign of human habitation was an occasional herd of cattle grazing along a drying creek bed or the distant glimpse of an isolated ranch.

Earlier that month, the four had been elected to represent the people of Los Angeles at the state constitutional convention in Monterey. To bring the delegates from the southern districts to the capital, the military governor had ordered the steamer *Edith* sent south; however, she had been lost on the treacherous rocks at Point Conception, so now the four men had started their long journey on horseback.

Like the other delegates from all over California who were converging on Monterey, they represented a variety of backgrounds. Stephen Clark Foster had come west as translator with the Mormon Battalion and was later appointed the first American *alcalde* of Los Angeles. With considerably more wisdom and understanding than many of his fellow appointees, he had served only one term, then called an election so that the citizens could choose local officials. Now the grateful Californians had returned the confidence by selecting him to represent them at Monterey.

In contrast, the merchant Abel Stearns had been a resident of California for twenty years. Married into one of the old Spanish families, he had been one of the men entrusted with Thomas Larkin's secret plans to stir up a bloodless revolution among the Californians. It had also been Stearns who had sent that first shipment of California gold to the United States Mint from Don Francisco Lopez' claim, in 1843.

The other two delegates were native Californians: José Carrillo, the fiery military leader who had led the Californians at the Battle of the Old Woman's Gun, and Luis Dominguez, on whose rancho outside of Los Angeles the battle had been fought.

"I have the feeling that when the Americans see me in Monterey, they may wish that the *Edith* had waited until her return voyage to go down, when she had us aboard," Carrillo observed wryly.

"The war is over now, Don José," Foster protested. "Besides, that is not the American way. The governor sent word to hold an election, not whom to elect. We would form a poor excuse of a state if you native Californians were not represented."

"That is just it. I am not certain that I am in favor of forming a state," Carrillo said. "We in the south have little in common with all these Americans who are rushing to the gold fields. I say let them form a state if they wish, but let us go our way and form a territory."

"You have not been an American long enough, Don José, to know that there are more advantages to living in a state than in a territory," Stearns explained. Then his long, rather plain face clouded. "But I must admit that I have worries too. To operate any government takes revenue, and I am wondering how our new state plans to raise money. The miners in the north have all the gold, but they do not pay taxes. It would not be fair to tax only the landowners. In fact, I am even wondering if anyone is going to pay us for this long trip," he added peevishly.

The others exchanged amused glances. Stearns had not become the wealthiest merchant in Los Angeles by being careless with his money.

"Taxes, statehood . . . these things do not worry me as much as the land itself," Dominguez said. "When we signed the agreement at Cahuenga, the American, Frémont, promised we could keep our land grants; but again and again we have asked the military governor for some proof of our holdings without any success. Maybe once we are a state, our land claims will be settled."

"And what good will land titles do if we have another drought and our cattle die?" Carrillo asked. "If we must worry, let it be about things that are important, señores. Do not tell me these Americans are so shrewd that they can legislate the weather too?"

The others laughed. As they continued on, they talked in fluent Spanish, not of gold, citizens' committees or booming real estate values, but of cattle, hides, rainfall and fast horses, those topics that had been the favorites of Californians for generations.

In 1848 the United States and England had settled their boundary dispute at the forty-ninth parallel, and Oregon had entered the union as a territory. At the same time, California had been refused territorial standing on the grounds that it would be unfair to the American-born Oregonians to give a bunch of Mexicans equal status. Fortunately, the citizens of California were too busy with their gold rush throughout most of 1848 to take affront at this insult, but in 1849 things changed. The Forty-niners had enjoyed all the privileges of citizenship back home, and they arrived in California demanding these same rights. Meanwhile, as witnessed in San Francisco, the expanding population made it evident that the existing government was no longer adequate.

In some of the larger towns the citizens showed their

dissatisfaction by holding town meetings of protest, one meeting in Sacramento going as far as to try to create a legislative assembly with Peter Burnett, a popular lawyer and former Oregonian, as president. In 1849, Brigadier General Bennett Riley replaced Colonel Richard Mason as military governor of California. When Congress adjourned again that year without having taken any action on the California question, Governor Riley personally issued orders for the constitutional convention to be held at Monterey. As a result of the gold rush, a year after being denied status as a territory, California was ready to leapfrog straight to statehood without going through any period of territorial government.

The state was divided into ten districts to send thirty-seven delegates to the convention: five each from San Francisco, Monterey and San Jose; four from Sacramento, Sonoma, San Joaquin and Los Angeles; and two from San Luis Obispo, Santa Barbara and San Diego; however, an additional clause stated that any district not feeling it was adequately represented could send more. While the southern, cattle-raising districts sent exactly the ten delegates allotted them, the northern mining districts chose eleven extra, giving them an overpowering majority.

Like the delegates from Los Angeles, many were men who already had taken part in California's history. The roster included such names as John Sutter, Thomas Larkin, John Bidwell and Robert Semple. Of the eight native Californians, Carrillo and General Mariano Vallejo were the most prominent. Among the few Forty-niners elected delegates, William Gwin, a politician from Tennessee, was outstanding. Gwin had come west with the announced intention of taking the lead in California politics; but in spite of this personal ambition, his superior knowledge of parliamentary procedure made him a valuable asset.

It was September 4 before the meeting really got under way. The convention was held on the second floor of Colton

Hall, the new schoolhouse erected by *alcalde* Walter Colton. A single upstairs room, twenty-five feet wide by sixty feet long, was divided by a rail across the center to separate spectators from delegates. Big Robert Semple was elected president and took his place at the rostrum at the end of the room. Behind him, displayed against the wall, were two American flags and an imaginative portrait of George Washington as conceived by a local artist. The other delegates took places at four long tables where William Gwin had placed a printed copy of the new Iowa state constitution on each seat. Later, the New York constitution would also be consulted.

Though old-timers in respect to California's history, the delegates were far from old in years. Only four were over fifty; the majority still in their twenties and thirties. With the exception of Gwin, few had any previous experience in government. Yet in six weeks, in spite of their youth, inexperience and language barrier with their eight Spanish-speaking members, they created a remarkably sound constitution, so sound that it later would be the model for the constitution of Argentina.

On only one issue was there any real debate. On the north, south and west, California's boundaries were already determined by Oregon, Mexico and the Pacific Ocean. The question was how far east the new state should extend. Though the Spaniards had occupied only a narrow coastal strip, it was generally accepted that the area called "Alta California," acquired from Mexico, included everything east from the Pacific to the frontiers of the United States. William Gwin headed a faction who wished to follow these traditional lines and place the eastern boundary at the Rockies.

"You can't cut a territory into small pieces. Congress will never approve. The only way we will get the state admitted is to include all of old Alta California," Gwin argued.

Semple led the fight for a smaller state extending only to

the Sierra Nevada. "This is the area where we live. What do we want with all that extra land?" was his argument.

Despite Gwin's superior political acumen, the majority preferred Semple's logic. "We've all heard that Brigham Young and his Mormons want to form a state of their own called Deseret. We can't include them in California when they aren't even represented at the convention," someone argued.

Shrewd businessmen such as Larkin and Stearns presented an even more convincing argument. "The moment we extend our boundaries to the Rockies we become responsible for the protection of every emigrant crossing the desert. Now where are we going to find troopers and money for a job like that?"

The result was a compromise on the present boundary of California, with the Sierra Nevada Mountains the dividing point, the border set to the east of them so that they too were included within the state.

Saturday, October 13, was the final day of the convention. The night before, the citizens of Monterey had entertained the delegates at a dance in honor of the occasion, so that when the delegates took their seats the hall was still draped with pine boughs and bedraggled streamers left from the night before.

Robert Semple was ill that morning, and it seemed fitting that John Sutter, the beloved "Old Gentleman," be appointed to preside over this final session. The morning business consisted principally of fiscal matters; then at twelve thirty the convention was briefly adjourned. At one o'clock it reconvened, and Semple, who had arrived by now, escorted Military Governor Riley into the hall where he placed his signature on the constitution. A signal was given from the window, outside the American flag was run up, and from the fort the cannon began a salute.

Overcome with emotion, Sutter leaped to his feet. "Gentlemen, this is the happiest day of my life . . . this is a great day for California!" he cried, his eyes filled with tears.

As he sat down the delegates replied with a cheer; then while the cannonade continued they too signed the document. The cannon sounded thirty times for the thirty states of the Union, then boomed once more.

"That's the shot for California!" an exuberant delegate cried, and Colton Hall resounded with more cheers.

Anxious to return to their homes, many of the delegates left Monterey that afternoon. "What do you think of our new constitution?" Stearns asked Carrillo as they returned to their lodgings.

In the fervor of the convention, Carrillo had relinquished his idea of creating a southern territory. "I think it is a splendid document," he agreed enthusiastically. Then some of his native skepticism returned, "Let us just hope that it works."

With the same optimism with which they had ordered a salute of thirty-one guns, the Californians proceeded to set up their state government without waiting for congressional approval. An election for the ratification of the constitution and selection of state representatives was set for November, with the first legislature scheduled to meet a month later.

Though outspoken in demanding their rights as citizens, few Forth-niners had any intentions of remaining in California or had any interest in local politics. Out of a total population of 100,000, California had almost 80,000 eligible male voters; yet only 12,875 went to the polls on November 13. But out of that number, 12,064 overwhelmingly approved the new constitution. Peter Burnett, the same lawyer whom the Sacramentans had chosen earlier to head their legislative assembly, was elected governor.

In December, without having received any word from Washington, the state legislature went ahead and met for the first time. The inspiration shown by the constitutional delegates at Monterey did not extend to this first legislature. Their principal achievements were choosing William Gwin and John Frémont as U.S. Senators, voting themselves salaries, passing a bigoted tax on foreign miners that would cost the state untold grief, and winning the derogatory title of the "Legislature of a Thousand Drinks," because of their frequent motions to adjourn for refreshments.

In Washington, D.C., the question of California's admission as a state precipitated a national crisis. Gwin had argued that the state's size would influence its admission, but Congress could not have cared less about boundaries. What concerned them was one small sentence tucked into the constitution by unanimous agreement of the delegates: ". . . neither slavery nor involuntary servitude, unless for the punishment of crimes, shall ever be tolerated in this state."

The United States had thirty states which were equally divided, fifteen free and fifteen slave. The admission of California as a free state would shift this balance of power. Since 1820 the Missouri Compromise, an imaginary line drawn at 36 degrees 30 minutes above which slavery was prohibited, had managed to keep the mounting differences between North and South in check; but the Missouri Compromise was useless now, for if extended westward to the Pacific the line would cut the new state in half.

President Zachary Taylor favored the speedy admission of California on its own merits with a complete reappraisal of the slavery issue to be taken up later; but the South had no intentions of allowing such a concession to the North. It is doubtful if many Southerners really opposed California's statehood, but it offered a means to bargain with the North; and to relieve the crisis, Henry Clay offered a compromise bill linking the admission of California with the entire slavery question. For weeks, then months, the debate raged, but because the compromise contained so many provisions it was impossible to get it approved.

In 1850 both John Calhoun, the leading orator for the South, and President Taylor died in office. In March 1850, Daniel Webster stunned the nation by abandoning his traditional position with the North to urge signing of the compromise as the only means to save the Union, but still the controversy continued. A year had passed since the four delegates had ridden north from Los Angeles to the constitutional convention at Monterey, and Congress still labored.

Shortly before October of 1850, the citizens of San Francisco had changed the name of Alta Loma to Telegraph Hill. From the top of this hill it was possible to see the entrance to the bay, and an observation tower had been erected in 1849 so that a lookout could signal the town below whenever a ship entered the Golden Gate. However, the merchants and businessmen wished to have news of approaching vessels before they were actually inside the harbor, so in 1850 a second observation tower was erected on the coast at Point Lobos and connected by California's first telegraph line with the first tower on Telegraph Hill. Now as soon as an approaching vessel appeared above the horizon, the news was flashed inland to Telegraph Hill, where the operator rushed from his shack and raised the arms of a semaphore, alerting the townspeople to the approach of the ship and the type of vessel.

On October 18, 1850, the semaphore tower was still enough of a novelty so that when its great arms began to stir, everyone stopped on the streets to look. As the black arms slowly raised opposite each other, then tilted slightly skyward in a supplicating position, a shout went up from below: "Sidewheel steamer!" If it had been a mere sailing ship most of the people would have continued about their work, but the twice monthly arrival of the mail steamer was an important event. While the adults of the town rushed to the docks, the usual crowd of small boys scrambled up Telegraph Hill to catch the first glimpse of the mail ship.

Today the *Oregon* was a sight to behold. She entered the harbor with whistles blowing and ribbons flying from every railing and porthole. Once inside, she unfurled several long, printed banners from her superstructure. It did not matter that the bay breezes whipped them so violently that the people could barely read the letters, only one event could have caused such a spectacle . . . CALIFORNIA A STATE . . . THIRTY-FIRST IN THE UNION . . . STATEHOOD!

On September 9, 1850, President Millard Fillmore had finally put his signature on the bill making California a state. People hugged each other and danced in the streets. Couriers were dispatched to spread the news to the mining camps, and for almost two weeks all of California was a scene of riotous celebration.

In Washington, D.C., there were few joyous faces. Clay's compromise bill had not been passed as one unit, but it had been necessary to pass most of it to secure California's admission. The same day that California became a state, President Fillmore also signed bills guaranteeing Utah and New Mexico "squatters' sovereignty," or the right to decide whether they would be slave or free on their admission to the union, a concession to the South. A few days later he also signed the Fugitive Slave Bill, requiring the return of runaway slaves and prohibiting them jury trial, another concession to the South. Many in the North believed that the price paid for California's admission had been too dear. An equal number of Southerners would never forgive the bitterness and hatred engendered by that long year of debate. The controversy over California's admission had left a rift between North and South that would never be completely bridged again, that would only widen in the decade ahead, leading eventually to the Civil War.

XI

The Restless Hills

THE GOLD FEVER WAS NOT CONFINED TO THE UNITED States alone. In France it was not even necessary to come to California to share in the bonanza. Promoters wishing to stir French interest in the gold rush melted one hundred pounds of nuggets into a single ingot which was sent to France. Displayed throughout the nation, it aroused such interest that a lottery was organized to send deserving young Frenchmen to California, while the winners split the gold of the ingot. In addition to a first prize of eighty thousand dollars, there were two hundred lesser prizes, and several thousand youths were provided free transportation to the gold fields. Despite the fact that France also used the sailing lists to rid herself of some political undesirables, the "Ingots," as they were called, succeeded in the mines and many struck it rich.

By 1850 a census showed that one quarter of California's population came from a foreign country. As the hills became more crowded and competition for gold grew keener, feelings rose against these foreigners, who many Americans felt were sharing riches that were not rightfully theirs.

Because the majority of the foreign-born they had known back in the eastern states were of European extraction, the American Forty-niners did not particularly resent the European miner; but one unique feature of the gold rush was that it brought to the United States for the first time, an influx of emigrants from Mexico, South America and China. Because their ways seemed strange, these newcomers drew the brunt of the prejudice.

First on the scene, the Hispanic miners were also first to feel the discrimination. There were a number of reasons for this dislike. Some was hatred that still lingered from the recent Mexican War. Because many from Mexico, Chile and Peru had been experienced miners in their homeland, they frequently succeeded in finding gold while the novice American failed. Finally, though the majority were hardworking and honest, they also included a ruffian element who by 1850 had turned some of the towns of the Southern Mines into the most lawless in the state.

Though it included all foreigners, the Foreign Miners Tax passed by the state legislature in 1850 was aimed principally at the Hispanic miner. It imposed a tax of twenty dollars a month, an amount that many could not pay. Each spring thousands of miners from Sonora, Mexico, trekked north like gypsies over Anza's old trail to work in the gold fields during the warm months, then returned home to Mexico with the coming of winter. Many brought their families with them. With the passing of the tax many of these law-abiding miners, not wishing any trouble for their families, packed up quietly and left the gold fields never to return.

Among the tougher element who stayed on, it was a different story. Though the tax had been levied, no practical means had been set up for collecting it, and they simply refused to pay.

Some camps went so far as to pass laws banning Mexicans, South Americans and Asiatics. This did not always work either, particularly in the case of the aristocratic Dr. Concha, who mined near Mokelumne Hill using peon labor he had brought with him from Chile. Instead of being intimidated when the Americans passed a law banning Chileans, Dr. Concha armed fifty men and marched on the Americans to arrest those who were harassing him. In the fray that followed, two Americans were killed and a dozen others seized as hostages. An army of enraged American miners was rallied from neighboring camps, but before the incident, known as the Chilean War, was settled there were more casualties on both sides. In the end Dr. Concha was defeated by superior numbers, several of his men were hanged, the rest had their ears cropped and were banished; but the incident created even more bitterness, and some of the more responsible California citizens began to fear reprisals against Americans living in South American countries.

A few of the miners did not wait to return to their homeland but found vengeance right in the gold fields. The most notable among these was the famous bandit, Joaquin Murieta. Romanticized over the years in novels and movies, the real story of Murieta has become wrapped in such a cocoon of legend that today it is practically impossible to sort fact from fiction. His fame was so widespread and he had so many imitators that old records have blamed him for raids and murders on the same day at towns hundreds of miles apart. Historians even disagree on the spelling of his name, some preferring Murrietta or Murietta; however, a few facts seem indisputable.

It is generally accepted that Murieta arrived in California in 1849 as a youth in his late teens. It is believed that he and his girl friend, Rosita, were in San Francisco the night that the Hounds made their infamous raid on Little Chile; but it is known for a certainty that a short time later he was mining in the Stanislaus region. Here most accounts say that a band of ruffians fell on his camp, stole his gold, and attacked and murdered Rosita. Others add that Murieta also saw his half-brother hanged and he himself was flogged for a crime he did not commit.

Whatever his motives, there is little doubt of his hatred of Americans. Surrounded by a gang of cutthroat bandits, he soon was leading raids on miners' camps, ranches and towns throughout the length of California. His second in command was Manuel Garcia, better known as Three-Fingered Jack, a notorious criminal with a record of murder dating back to the days of the Bear Flag Revolt. The object of the raids was always robbery but the results were frequently mass murder. Murieta was rumored to carry a string of human ears hung from his saddlehorn, and Three-Fingered Jack was reported to be even more bloodthirsty.

There is no historical evidence that Murieta was the Robin Hood character that fiction has depicted him as. If his fellow countrymen hid him out, one suspects they were motivated more by fear than affection.

The fact that Murieta liked to gamble gave rise to a favorite story told at several camps. One night the miners in a gambling hall got to talking about the famous bandit, and one boastfully threw a poke containing five hundred dollars on the table. "I'll bet my last ounce of dust if I ever meet that rascal, Murieta, I'll kill him on sight," he bragged.

A dark, dapper-looking man, who had been sitting at the next table all evening, rose abruptly and his hand closed around the bag. "I'll take that bet, señor, and Joaquin Murieta thanks you." Before the startled miners could recover, the bandit was out of the door and on his horse, his famed cry, "I am Joaquin," floating back through the night.

At the mining camp of Murphys, Murieta was supposed to have a favorite Mexican barber. Whenever he came into town Murieta would stride into the barber shop, throw himself into the chair and announce in a fierce voice, "I'll pay you well for a shave, but if you so much as nick me, I'll kill you."

Whereupon the little barber would nod and smile and proceed confidently about his work. Finally, the barber's best friend could stand it no longer. "How can you suffer such an ordeal time after time? How can you keep your hand from trembling when you know you are only seconds from death?" he asked.

"Why should my hands tremble when I know that Murieta will never kill me?" the barber replied.

"But Murieta is a man who means what he says!" the friend protested.

"I know," the barber snapped impatiently. "That is why I decided long ago what I must do if I ever should be so unfortunate as to nick Murieta's cheek. The razor will already be in my hand. Quick before he can leap from the chair, I will slash his throat." The barber patted his small, deadly edged razor. "No, *amigo,* it is not I but the great *bandito* who should pray that my hand remains steady."

Such tales as these make up the legend of Murieta but it was a fact that by May 1853, he had become such a scourge that the state legislature authorized Captain Harry Love to organize a band of state troopers to go into the hills and put an end to the depredations. Six weeks later, the citizens of California breathed a sigh of relief as the newspapers reported that the troopers had caught up with Murieta and some of his men in the Tulare Valley and accomplished their mission. In the running fight, Murieta, Three-Fingered Jack and several others had been killed while three of the party had escaped. As proof, Captain Love cut off Murieta's head; and the grisly trophy, along with the hand of Three-Fingered Jack, was preserved in a jar and exhibited publicly.

Yet even Murieta's death had an element of mystery. The *Alta Californian,* one of San Francisco's leading newspapers, went along with the rest of the press in reporting the death, but a few weeks later its editor printed a retraction saying that it now had been learned from the three men who had escaped that it had not been Murieta who had been killed at Tulare Valley but an imitator, Joaquin Valenzuela.

Whether it was Murieta whom Captain Love had killed, or whether the real bandit, taking warning from the incident, fled into Mexico, the raids stopped; and the legislature was sufficiently satisfied to vote Captain Love a reward of five thousand dollars.

By 1853 the Spanish-speaking miner had ceased to be a problem, for emigration from Mexico and the South American countries had stopped almost completely.

The year 1850 only added to San Francisco's growing pains as the city struggled to keep pace with the hordes of miners who continued to arrive by sea and the thousands more drifting back from the mines. Tent structures gave way to row after row of wooden buildings, many of them ready-made houses sent around the Horn from New York. Newly constructed wharfs and piers jutted out into the bay; and to avoid another winter of mud such as that of 1849, sidewalks of wooden planking were laid down. Everywhere above the voices of the noisy elbowing throngs on the street, one heard the steady pounding of hammers.

San Francisco had to keep building. The fire of December 1849 had been only a foretaste of trouble to come. In May, June and September of 1850, the city was swept by three more great fires, and the spring of 1851 brought little relief as the newly organized, volunteer fire companies were called out for a rash of smaller blazes that continued to erupt almost daily. The fires were inevitably accompanied by looting. At first it had been easy to blame the blazes on the tinderbox construction of the city, but with each rebuilding, the houses had become more substantial. As the fires continued, in many citizens' minds came the dawning and terrible realization that they were being set as a cover for crime.

In 1849 Brannan's Committee of Safety had driven out the Hounds, but they had not dealt with the Sydney Ducks, the Australian convict element that overflowed from Sydney Town on the waterfront to envelope the city in a new wave of terror. Murders and robberies were daily occurrences. Few criminals were apprehended, and those who were arrested were rarely convicted.

Shortly before midnight on May 3, 1851, the citizens of San Francisco were again awakened by the clamor of fire bells. That they had become a familiar sound did not lessen their terror; but tonight's blaze, which had started in a paint and upholstery shop off the plaza, was to be one all would remember.

By the time the Howard Volunteers could pull their ornate, silver-trimmed engine down Montgomery Street and join the boys of the Monumental and California Companies, who were already pumping, a gust of wind had swept the flames across Kearny Street and out of control. Men with buckets, blankets and axes joined the volunteers, but their efforts were useless. At one point they almost seemed to have the blaze under control when suddenly a building four doors away erupted in a pillar of flames. Barely had crews rushed to this new blaze than a house at the end of the block ignited. For a moment, there were cries that arsonists were still at work, until the men discovered their true enemy was the elevated sidewalk that they had installed so proudly. The air space beneath the wooden planking served as a roaring chimney that sucked the fire underground to burst out elsewhere in flaming geysers.

Even blasting powder did not work. As the holocaust mounted, the fire leaped the explosion-leveled areas. The heat became so intense that the water from the fire hoses turned to vapor, buildings of brick crumbled, and iron doors and shutters expanded trapping terrified victims inside.

That night the residents of Monterey, a hundred miles to the south, witnessed an awesome sight. Reflected in the overhanging clouds of the night sky, they saw the fiery glow of California's largest city going up in flames. The following day when the blaze was finally contained, two thousand buildings and most of San Francisco's business district had burned.

The following month there would be still another fire, which would satisfy its appetite with sixteen square blocks of residences; but before this happened the aroused citizens had taken matters into their own hands.

"The Sydney Ducks are behind this. It isn't enough to rob and murder us, now they want to burn us out too!" Sam Brannan protested testily to his friends.

"We can't expect any help from the sheriff. The only way we'll stop the fires and looting and murder is to organize, like we did in forty-nine," someone added.

Circumstances had changed in two years. It was no longer possible for Brannan to simply roll a barrel into the center of Montgomery Street and harangue the townspeople. San Francisco was a city now. For such an undertaking to be successful it must be planned and executed with an air of responsibility.

In early June a letter appeared in the *Alta Californian* suggesting that the citizens unite, followed by several editorials in the same vein; yet none were couched in such inflammatory language as to warn the citizens that anything actually was afoot. Only a few curious observers noticed that an unusual number of men seemed to be going into the California Company firehouse on June 9, while the following day, June 10, even more found some reason to transact business with Brannan in his offices on Bush Street.

That evening around ten o'clock, San Francisco was startled by the ringing of the fire bell. This time it had a different sound: not the wild continuous clamor that signaled a fire, but repeated, short peals that had a special urgency of their own. Some citizens seemed to know what the odd signal meant. In houses up near Telegraph Hill family men hastily donned their coats; downtown others excused themselves from card games or bid good-night to companions in the saloons.

On June 9, Brannan and a group of former members of the

1849 committee had organized a new Committee of Vigilance, with a written constitution and bylaws, and had elected officers. Members were sworn to secrecy, assigned numbers instead of names, and alerted that the ringing of the Monumental Firehouse bell would be their signal for assembly.

Tonight before the weary executive committee had completed registering all the applicants, an armed patrol had brought in the first prisoner, John Jenkins, a notorious Sydney Duck with a long list of unpunished crimes to his discredit. The ringing of the bell had been a summons to members for the first trial.

Jenkins, who had been caught stealing a safe, was scornful and sneering. "You can't do anything. My friends are going to break in here and release me, and if they don't the sheriff will," he bragged.

"String him up and let him be an example to the others!" one of the vigilantes cried angrily.

"That's the spirit, boy!" Colonel Stevenson, who had led the New York Volunteers to California in 1847, agreed exuberantly.

"To act in violence will make us no better than the criminals we are trying to punish. We may have been forced to step outside the law, but let us make our actions those of responsible men," a young merchant, William Coleman, cautioned. Though a relative newcomer, Coleman already had won widespread admiration for his forcefulness and cool thinking. The others agreed that they must act with caution, but when the trial was over and the prisoner found guilty, a vote showed that the majority still favored hanging.

A noisy crowd had gathered outside in the streets. Among them were many of Jenkins' criminal friends as well as more responsible citizens who were opposed to vigilante action. When Brannan started for the door to speak to them, several members tried to bar his way. "We're sworn to secrecy. If we let anyone know what we're doing, we'll have the local law officers down on us," someone warned.

"Bill Coleman just warned us to act like responsible citizens. If we truly believe in what we're doing, then I say we owe it to the public to let them know what we're about!" Brannan cried.

Inside the executive chamber, Coleman was the cool, logical thinker but Brannan was still San Francisco's most persuasive orator. "You like being burned out of your homes and businesses? You like walking down the street at night, trembling with fear every time you pass an alleyway because you know you may be knifed?" he roared to the crowd.

If Brannan did not win the agreement of the mob, at least he quieted them enough so that there was no protest when Jenkins was led from the headquarters at 2:00 A.M. Lacking a better gallows, it had been decided to hang him from one of the jutting beams of the customs house. The sheriff met them as they neared the plaza and demanded the prisoner. It was a token gesture. When the vigilantes refused, he disappeared angrily into the crowd.

Jenkins refused the services of a preacher. His last request as the noose was fitted around his neck was for a good cigar. In the face of such sneering nonchalance some of the vigilantes hesitated. Brannan sprang forward seizing the rope. "Lay on, every lover of liberty and good order! Lay on!" he cried.

The cigar fell from Jenkins' lips as fifty men seized the rope jerking him aloft. Afterward his body was left swinging from the beam as a grim warning.

The repercussions were immediate. Nine leading citizens were named by a coroner's inquest as responsible for the illegal act. In rebuttal, one hundred eighty vigilantes published their names in the newspaper claiming equal responsibility. Brannan had been right. Their willingness to stand openly behind their actions seemed to quiet the fears of the public. No action was brought, and for the next three months the vigilantes conducted their clean-up campaign virtually unopposed. In all about ninety persons were brought before them on warrants signed with the dread "67," the number of the committee's secretary, Isaac Bluxome, Jr. Three more were hanged, one flogged, fifteen turned over to the regular authorities, and the rest either deported or released. In late summer, their work finished and the city quiet again, the vigilantes disbanded.

In February 1848, the first three Chinese had arrived in California aboard the ship *Eagle* as the servants of a visiting couple from Hong Kong. The following year a few hundred more arrived, a few going to the mines but most setting up small businesses in San Francisco. By 1851 there were still only a few thousand of them; then in 1852, this number skyrocketed to twenty thousand.

In the beginning the Chinese was considered an oddity, more often the butt of a joke than a real threat. Peaceful, hard-working, able to live on the most meager rations, the great majority of them made their living working over claims abandoned by the Americans. Few had the independent means to reach California but came as contract labor for the great mercantile companies of China, who extracted a percentage of all that they made. The Chinese made no effort to mingle with the other miners or even learn English, but stayed by themselves in their Chinatowns on the edge of the mining camps where they continued to wear their long queues and the blue blouses and pantaloons of their homeland, so that their very strangeness made them seem suspect. They were never seen drunk in public, but whispers circulated about opium smoking and other strange practices that went on in their joss houses. They loved to gamble, but the Americans who ventured into their gambling halls usually came away heavy losers.

It was known that the average Chinese was very proud of his queue, a curious symbol of his difficulties under the Manchu dynasty, and it was a favorite sport of groups of toughs to threaten to cut off a Chinese miner's queue unless he gave them his gold. The wise Chinese prepared for this with two stocks of gold: a big one well hidden, and an old can stuffed with a smaller amount which he offered to his tormentors.

Ridiculed, driven from their claims, almost always the losers in any legal encounters, the Chinese accepted life with a stoicism that was difficult for the Western mind to understand. On the occasions when they were aroused to do battle, oddly enough it was usually among themselves.

By 1854 the town of Weaverville had a sizable Chinese population with a Chinatown consisting of four gambling halls, four stores and one restaurant. One morning in early July, John Carr, a blacksmith, was startled when several Chinese came into his shop to order some fifteen-foot-long iron pikes. Though puzzled, Carr agreed to fashion them. "How many do you want . . . three, four?" he asked.

The Chinese exchanged looks. "Twenty," their spokesman said finally.

The next day several more Chinese came into the shop with orders for iron shields. This was followed by more orders: tube-shaped iron hats, three-pronged iron tridents, unwieldly five-foot swords with six-foot handles. By now the word was all over town that because of some real or fancied insult that the Americans never fully understood, the men of the Yangwah Company and those of the Canton Company had challenged each other to a war.

Soon Carr was hiring extra help to keep up with orders, but when the members of the two companies began parading in the street with their weapons, the sheriff decided that he should do something.

"Carr, you keep on making these crazy things and I'm going to arrest you for making weapons intended to do bodily harm, and that's a five-hundred-dollar offense."

"Go ahead and arrest me, Sheriff," Carr replied with a grin. "I can pay the five hundred dollars and still come out with a profit, and you'll find the same is true with every other blacksmith and hardware merchant in town."

The sheriff didn't know what to do, never having dealt with a war before. Finally he decided to do nothing, for the consensus of the townspeople seemed to be that if the Chinese wanted to kill themselves that was their business.

The battle was scheduled for July 14, and the night before, the opposing armies marched out of town to a meadow a mile away. In the morning while six hundred fifty Chinese assembled for the fight, two thousand miners flocked to watch. The Yangwah forces, dressed in red and carrying a white banner, numbered only one hundred fifty, but they charged first, then wheeled suddenly and marched back and forth displaying their weapons, including several enormous squirt guns filled with some evil-looking liquid.

Next the Canton forces, dressed in black and red and five hundred strong, made a charge. Only feet away from the enemy, they dropped to their knees and froze like statues brandishing their weapons. These false charges and posturings kept up all morning. It was three in the afternoon when the Yangwahs suddenly made a charge that was in earnest.

Caught by surprise, the Cantons momentarily fell back, then rallied half their force to encircle the smaller army. The wily leader of the Yangwahs had prepared for this. A steep hill protected his men on one side, and prior to the battle he had bribed a number of miners to rush in, preventing attack on the other flank. The miners rushed forward as agreed, the remainder of the spectators following them to get a better view. Unable to make their way through the yelling miners to surround the enemy, the Cantons fell back again, and ten minutes later the battle was over with the Yangwahs victorious. Eight Chinese had been killed outright and several more desperately wounded.

It was discovered that a spectator had also been killed, and for several minutes there was wild talk of revenge until an eyewitness explained what had happened. In the heat of the battle the dead miner, who was a known troublemaker, had pulled out a gun and started firing into the mass of Chinese. Shocked at this brutality, a second miner had calmly drawn his own pistol and put a bullet through the first miner's head. The crowd quickly agreed that the bully had got exactly what he deserved for his unsportsmanlike conduct, and everyone headed happily back to town.

Later there was a similar war at the town of Chinese Camp, but despite these battles and the constant persecution, the Chinese continued to arrive. By 1855 there were fifty thousand. Soon they would make up half of the miners working in the gold fields, the largest foreign element in the state, and would become one of the greatest problems California faced as a result of the gold rush.

Strangers filled the hills now and most of the early pioneers had turned to new interests. Bidwell had given up his interest in Bidwell Bar to return to his ranch. Sutter, living at Hock Farm, was involved in endless litigation over his land. After four years of fruitless wandering, James Marshall gave up the search also.

Wandering from camp to camp he had become more moody and withdrawn with each passing month. Once Sutter had loaned him a couple of Indian servants, but within a few days they had run away, saying they were afraid of this strange man who talked to himself. He could not even find work at his old trade. "Hire you? Why do you want a job when you can find gold?" people scoffed.

Finally in desperation he tried to make a living traveling about the country giving lectures and selling his autograph.

When this too proved unproductive, he retired to his small cabin at Coloma, with his bitter memories.

When the editor of a newspaper asked for his photograph Marshall refused, peevishly saying it was all that he had left of value in an unappreciative world: "The sale of it someday may yet keep me from starving, or may buy me a dose of medicine in sickness or pay for the funeral of a dog, and such is all that I expect, judging from former kindness."

Eventually granted a small pension by the state, he lived on in near poverty until his death in 1885, when he was buried on a hill at Coloma near the place where he had made his discovery. If the huge bronze statue of a miner that stands above his grave, with finger pointing to the exact spot where the first gold was found, seems of more heroic proportions than the man himself, one must remember that James Marshall was a simple, ordinary man who had not asked for this role that history had thrust upon him.

XII

The Bubble Bursts

PRIOR TO JAMES MARSHALL'S DISCOVERY THE UNITED States had been insignificant as a gold-producing nation. From 1851 to 1853 she produced 45 percent of the gold output of the world. The effect of such a shifting of wealth was felt in every nation, but nowhere more than in the United States itself, faced with the problem of creating better supply lines with this vast new source of riches. Daily, Aspinwall's railway penetrated deeper into the jungle at the Isthmus of Panama; but it would not be completed until 1855 and even then the fastest service it could offer would be four months from coast to coast. The answer seemed to be a transcontinental railway, with primary surveys favoring a southern route which would be open all year round. With this in mind the United States made the Gadsden Purchase in 1853, acquiring 45,535 acres of land from Mexico for ten million dollars and extending New Mexico and Arizona southward to their present border. Included in the purchase to become part of Arizona now was Tubac the tiny frontier outpost from which Anza had started northwest with the first settlers for California. Yet even while legislators labored at the steps to give the infant state closer ties to the Union, on the West Coast the golden bubble had begun to deflate.

With the exception of the Chinese, emigration from foreign countries fell off sharply in 1853. Though gold seekers continued to arrive from the other states, their numbers were matched now by miners leaving the gold fields to return home. For three years gold had been king, governing every decision, frequently to the detriment of good sense. Nowhere was this more evident than in the state government. After a series of childish squabbles that saw the state capital moved from one city to another, Sacramento was finally agreed upon as a permanent choice. It turned out to be one of the few matters upon which the legislators were able to agree. With the representatives of the northern, gold counties outnumbering those from the southern, cattle counties forty-four to twelve, almost all the legislation and appropriations favored the mining camps. When taxation was levied in just the opposite ratio, with the southern counties paying the larger share, José Carrillo and the fiery leader Andres Pico led a movement to withdraw from the state and set up an independent territory. Added to their grievances was the prejudiced settlement of the old Spanish land claims.

At the Capitulation of Cahuenga, Frémont had promised the Californians that they could keep their land, but that had been prior to the discovery of gold. In spite of Frémont's protests as a senator from California, Congress set up a Land Commission in 1851 before which the Californians were required to present proof of their claims. Some could not provide satisfactory proof. Others had prejudiced judges make decisions in favor of the newly arrived squatters or became involved in lawsuits with the government that dragged on for years.

Of all the claimants in the land courts, probably none suffered more than Sutter. Some of his land dated back to Mexican claims, some had been purchased from the Russians; he had sold farms here and there to American settlers and city lots to Sacramento businessmen. The result was a tangle few courts could have settled, and the majority of the decisions went against him.

Only one good seemed to have come to Sutter out of the

gold rush. Prior to 1848, though his wealth appeared tremendous, it had all been in land and stock; he had never possessed enough actual gold to bring his family from Switzerland. The sale of lots in Sacramento in 1849 finally gave him enough cash to send for the wife and children he had not seen for seventeen years, though by the time they arrived he was living at Hock Farm and his empire was crumbling. Yet, even this joy of reunion was short-lived. His children felt few ties to a father who was a virtual stranger, and soon married and moved away, leaving Sutter with only his wife.

At the same time that Sutter brought claims against the United States government, some of his titles were found worthless, and people to whom he had sold land brought claims against him. Legal fees claimed more of his dwindling wealth. Finally in 1865 Hock Farm burned to the ground, and with nothing left in California, Sutter and his wife moved to Lititz, Pennsylvania, where he hoped the hot baths would bring relief from the arthritis from which he now suffered. Several years later, learning he was penniless, a sympathetic state legislature voted him a pension of two hundred fifty dollars a month. The remainder of his life was spent in petitioning Congress for redress for his lost fortune. On June 18, 1880, Sutter died at age seventy-seven, alone in a Washington, D.C., hotel room where he had gone to present his petition just one more time.

If the state government was inadequate, city government, particularly in San Francisco, was openly corrupt. Respectable businessmen were too busy amassing fortunes to bother with politics. Sam Brannan, himself, was an example. By now his real estate investments had made him California's first millionaire, but though he had rallied his fellow citizens to action twice when their homes and businesses seemed threatened, he had refused a part in the constitutional convention at Monterey on the grounds that his business interests were too pressing. As a result of this widespread apathy, the city government became almost unbelievably corrupt: elections were fixed, city expenses skyrocketed, officials drew outrageous salaries. Crime increased and a horde of clever but unscrupulous lawyers descended on the city making it virtually impossible to get a conviction for any crime from embezzlement to murder.

At least one good had come to San Francisco out of the six great fires. No longer a maze of tents and jerry-built shacks, with each rebuilding its buildings had become more elaborate and substantial. It was a cosmopolitan city whose women dressed lavishly in silks and brocades from China. In 1849 Stephan Masset, an English baritone, had presented San Francisco with its first professional entertainment; but by the 1850's world-renowned performers such as Edwin Booth, Kate Hayes, Adah Mencken, Christy's Minstrels and the fiery Lola Montez flocked to the coast to appear in new theaters like the Jenny Lind, Adelphi, American, Bush Street Music Hall and Maquire's Opera House. The more affluent citizens gave up their homes at the base of Telegraph Hill and moved out to an exclusive new district called South Park, whose ornate iron fences and geometrically plotted rose gardens were reputed to be exact replicas of those of London's fashionable Berkeley Square.

Yet beneath this new aura of opulence and respectability was an undercurrent of restlessness. In the winter of 1853 as thousands of miners streamed down from the hills, for the first time San Francisco did not have jobs for those who were discouraged and out of work. In 1857 all of the nation would go through a depression brought about by the collapsing postwar boom, but in California where the gold fever was growing a little tarnished now, it came earlier. In 1854 Page, Bacon and Company, the great banking concern of St. Louis, closed its doors. The run on its Pacific Coast branches caused many other San Francisco banks to fail also, some maneuvering funds at the last moment so that a few big stockholders were protected while the small depositors lost everything.

That same year San Francisco suffered another devastating shock. Along with Brannan, "Honest Harry" Meiggs had continued to reign as one of the city's favorite benefactors. Hundreds held jobs because of him; he had built Meiggs Wharf, organized the first Philharmonic Association, and given the city the Bush Street Music Hall. He had served as a city alderman, his brother was currently city comptroller, and almost any citizen would tell you that the two of them were probably the only honest men in politics.

In spite of the fact that the city continued to spread southward, Meiggs never lost faith in his North Beach property, believing that eventually the city would have to expand that way to find deep-water anchorage for its increased shipping. Even when the city settled this problem by building a mile-long wharf that reached into deep water, Meiggs refused to give up.

Few people realized how much money Meiggs had put into North Beach or lost in the bank failures. In those days the city paid its debts with promissory notes signed by the mayor and comptroller, which were as negotiable as cash. No one was particularly surprised when Meiggs suddenly began to cash a great number of these notes, for he sold a great deal of lumber to the city. Nor were they surprised when he began to cash notes drawn on other local companies and borrow from his friends, though a few whispered that Honest Harry seemed to be spreading himself a little thin. Unknown to his friends, Meiggs had also contacted the owner of the sailing ship *American* and had her stocked with a two-year supply of the finest wines and foods. One evening early in October the captain of the *American* was summoned hastily to Meiggs' home. Both Meiggs and his brother were there, and there were several large bags of gold on the table. "I'm sorry to give you such short notice, Captain, but we must sail on tonight's tide," Meiggs said tersely. After the captain had rushed away to make preparations, Meiggs and his brother took a carriage to an isolated section of the waterfront and rowed out to the ship.

The next morning San Francisco was stunned. Honest Harry Meiggs, who had sailed into their harbor in 1849 with the cargo of lumber they so badly needed, had sailed off again with three hundred thousand dollars of their money. The city's promissory notes had been stolen, the notes on other companies forged, the loans signed with no intention of repayment.

It would be satisfying to say that Henry Meiggs was punished; unfortunately just the opposite was true. After a brief stay in the South Seas, he sailed to South America, where he became a railroad tycoon, a public hero to the people of Peru and Chile for his construction of railroads over the Andes, and a multimillionaire. In the 1870's when he took some of his enormous fortune and paid off his San Francisco debts, a generous state legislature passed a special bill that would permit him to return to California without being prosecuted. The governor along with hundreds of small businessmen, laundresses, lumbermen and investors who had suffered from his actions were not quite so forgiving. The governor vetoed the bill and Meiggs died in Peru in 1877 without ever having secured permission to return.

The embezzlement by their favorite son Henry Meiggs stirred San Francisco out of some of its apathy, but it required another vigilante action in 1856, this time under the leadership of William Coleman, before the city finally rid itself of the criminal element and corrupt politicians and settled down to a mature acceptance of its civic responsibilities.

If the face of San Francisco was changing in 1854, so was that of the mining camps. The sturdy wooden buildings built by the miners who had stuck out the winter of '49 were gradually being replaced by even more lasting structures of brick and stone. The long arenas where whooping miners had witnessed gory bear and bull fights gave way to permanent theaters where traveling actors performed. Most of the camps still had their hanging trees, but they were used less and less frequently as settlements began to elect sheriffs and judges and a more responsible kind of justice moved into the hills. While many gold seekers headed home, others sent for wives and sweethearts, so that homes and schools and churches began to appear.

A rising, new merchant and tradesmen class gave a backbone of permanency to the towns. Some of these gold field storekeepers went on to found great business empires. When Mark Hopkins, who had come around the Horn aboard the *Pacific,* drove a wagonload of supplies up to Hangtown to start a grocery store, he had as neighbors young Philip Armour, whose butcher shop was the start of the great Armour meat packing business, and John Studebaker, who progressed from making miners' wheelbarrows to wagons and eventually became a pioneer in the auto industry.

Behind the collapse of the gold fever perhaps no one element was more important than the change taking place in the mining itself. From the one-man operation of pan and rocker, the miners had progressed to the Long Tom in 1849. Soon, to speed production, the Long Tom gave way to the sluice, which was actually little more than a number of Toms or sections of trough fitted together on a slight downhill pitch. The sluices, which ranged anywhere from a hundred to a thousand feet long, required a steady flow of water and crews of men to shovel in the pay dirt, with the flow shut off every week or ten days while the gold was gathered from the riffle bars. Next, miners discovered that by throwing handsful of quicksilver into the sluices it would amalgamate with the gold, carrying it to the bottom much more quickly and allowing less to escape. Later the two metals were easily separated again by a relatively simple process of heat reduction.

By 1852, to wash down more earth for their sluices, the miners began to turn to hydraulic mining with crews of ten and twelve men manning tremendous pressure hoses that melted entire hillsides within minutes. Sluice and hydraulic mining required such tremendous amounts of water that streams had to be diverted, water companies formed and miles of flumes and ditches constructed. By 1854, 4,493 miles of ditches supplied the mines, and little of the gold that reached the new San Francisco Mint that year represented the work of individual miners but came from the combined efforts of many.

However, it was the start of hard-rock mining that marked the end of the independent miner. From the gravel of the stream bed, to the dust of the hillside, to the great underlying veins in the bedrock of the mountains, the Forty-niner had traced the gold to its source. It was this vast underground wealth called the "mother lode" that would maintain California as a gold-producing state for years. Having been hard-rock miners in their homeland, as early as 1849 the Spanish-speaking miners in the Southern Mines were mining ore and crushing it in their crude mule-drawn *arrastras*. The *arrastra* was a circular granite basin around which a mule walked slowly turning a grinding device to pulverize the ore; sometimes it was in the form of a large grindstone, other times an arrangement of huge spokes which tumbled large boulders as they turned. Even when the ore had been ground to dust, the gold must still be separated by the usual methods, and to the American miners the process appeared painfully slow. As long as the hills continued to produce loose gold, they preferred their easier placer methods, but by 1855 they were turning to hard-rock mining too. But hard-rock mining required capital: it meant tunnels, shoring material, ore carts, machinery for stamp mills to crush the ore, power to drive the mills and quicksilver for the amalgamating process. Miners with money banded together to form companies, while those who had not fared so well went to work for others.

John C. Frémont was one of those paradoxical men whose life seemed a continual series of heights and depressions, on whom Fortune seemed to cast a dazzling light one moment and a shadow the next. As a famed explorer, supporter of the Bear Flag Revolt and leader of the California Battalion, Frémont appeared to be the top man in California in January of 1847. Before the year was out, having taken the wrong side in a contest between Navy Commodore Robert F. Stockton and Army General Stephen W. Kearny over who was the top authority in California, Frémont had been called back to Washington in disgrace to stand court-martial for having disobeyed the orders of his superior, General Kearny. Found guilty on two counts, Frémont resigned his commission in disgust and headed back to California where he had decided to make his home. Even his financial affairs appeared in a dismal state. Before leaving California to face the court-martial, he had given Thomas Larkin three thousand dollars to buy him a certain piece of ranch property just south of San Francisco Bay. Either through error or because he had a shrewd eye for real estate, Larkin bought the land for himself and sent Frémont the deed to another piece of property, a huge but seemingly worthless Mexican land grant one hundred miles inland in the foothills of the Sierras.

Frémont was justly furious; then before he could reach the coast to demand his money back, James Marshall made his discovery and Frémont arrived in California to find that his Mariposa grant contained some of the richest gold-bearing ore in the Southern Mines. Moreover, he arrived just in time to be elected United States Senator by the California state legislature on their first ballot. His star in the ascendancy again, Frémont swept back to Washington where he went on to become the Presidential candidate of the Republican party in 1856.

Frémont's political activities temporarily kept him from giving full attention to his mining property. Also, like all holders of Mexican land grants, he was required to present proof of his ownership before the Land Commission. Though the Land Commission approved the grant, a district court reversed the decision. It was not until 1855 that a decision handed down by the United States Supreme Court finally approved Frémont's title and set the boundaries of his land.

In 1857 following his defeat for the Presidency by James Buchanan, Frémont headed back to California to devote his full time to his Mariposa property. The following spring he was joined by his wife, Jessie, their daughter, Lily, their two small sons and two house guests: Frémont's nineteen-year-old niece, Nina, and a young English boy, Charles Fox, who was living with them while he learned the mining business.

Frémont was in another financial slump, and like many others of that day he lacked the capital to develop all of his property at once; but he went ahead as fast as he could, and by early summer his two small stamp mills were already producing close to three thousand dollars a month. However Frémont's arrival had not been greeted with enthusiasm by his neighbors. During the years he had been away, squatters had overrun his land. Now, those who remained had banded into companies. One group in particular, the Merced Mining Company, felt that the decision driving them off Frémont's land was unfair, and they brought suit against him, threatening physical violence if it wasn't settled to their liking.

Frémont heard of the mounting feeling against him through his workers, but he carefully refrained from worrying his wife and the others as they settled into their comfortable, white frame house overlooking the tiny village of Bear Valley and about three miles from the mines. The summer was hot but the family developed a retreat higher in the mountains where they often went for picnics; and since Frémont had a stable of spirited horses, the young people spent much of their time riding through the hills.

Then one morning Frémont and his wife were awakened by the sound of furiously galloping hoofbeats. Seconds later there was a heavy pounding on their bedroom window "Colonel . . . Colonel, there's trouble. The Merced boys have jumped the Black Drift!" a voice called.

"What's wrong? What is he saying?" Jessie sat up in alarm as Frémont flew across the room.

"Nothing, just mining matters. Go on back to sleep while I straighten them out," Frémont replied in a casual voice, motioning to the man outside the window to be silent.

However, there was nothing casual in Frémont's manner moments later as he raced from the back door to the stable where the rider was already saddling his horse. His worst fears had been realized. The Merced Company, taking advantage of a recent California court ruling that allowed miners to take possession of unoccupied claims, had marched on Frémont's property during the night, bribed the watchman at the Black Drift and taken possession of the mine. Three quarters of a mile away at the settlement of Bear Valley where most of his workers lived, Frémont received more bad news. Spreading out from their easy victory, the Merced Company had seized the Josephine shaft too and were on their way to another mine. Then a shout went up from the workers as a scout galloped into camp. "The Pine Tree is still ours! The boys at the Pine Tree have barricaded themselves and are holding them off!" he cried.

It was the first good news to arrive. Six men had been working at the Pine Tree mine. Alerted by the noise at the nearby Black Drift and Josephine they had taken refuge in the tunnel, where behind a fortress of machinery, kegs, boxes and sandbags they were successfully holding off the invaders with their rifles.

Taking only a few men with him and staying undercover, Frémont set out to look over the situation. All three mines were located partway up a steep hill, in front of them a small flattened clearing used for the turning of the ore wagons. The men of the Merced Company were well situated around the edges of this clearing now. If they could not take the Pine Tree, neither could the men inside receive any reinforcements. While Frémont had about twenty employees, the Merced forces had around seventy, many of them hired thugs and gunmen brought in for this job, while rumors had it they were signing up more as fast as they could hire them.

"First, we've got to send someone for help," Frémont said.

"We can't," one of his men replied. "They've placed guards across every road and trail."

Realizing that he could not keep the news from his family any longer, Frémont hurried home to tell them what had happened; but he tried to minimize the danger, warning them only that they were to stay in the house until the trouble was settled. His secret orders to the servants were more explicit. He had heard of some of the boasts the Merced Company men had made about what they planned to do to him and his family. "If the ruffians get past us, shoot the three women before you let them fall into the hands of that mob!" he said.

Seventeen-year-old Charles Fox overheard this order. His face pale, he caught up with Frémont at the door. "Let me ride for help, sir. I can get through their lines," he begged.

"You'd never make it. They have every road and trail well guarded."

"Lily, Nina and I have ridden the hills for weeks now. I know every inch of the country. I'll find my way past them by some secret path," Fox insisted.

Frémont studied him thoughtfully. "You might make it at that, lad," he said abruptly. At the stable, he personally selected his daughter's horse, Ayah, and saw young Fox off into the darkness.

Leading the horse, following animal paths and little-known trails, the boy made his way around the mountain, several times passing within a few hundred feet of the sentries. At last gaining the crest of the ridge, he dropped down the other side and raced Ayah along the banks of the Merced River into Coulterville where he notified the sheriff. Other messengers were dispatched to the capital at Sacramento.

Meanwhile back in Bear Valley, Frémont had not been idle. The men of the Merced Company had forgotten they were dealing with a military man. With only twenty men Frémont could not possibly attack the enemy, who now numbered close to a hundred; but while they were watching the mine entrance he brought his men up behind them, then with a volley of gunfire let them know where he was. If the six men besieged in the mine could not receive any reinforcements, neither could the men of the Merced Company, for Frémont controlled the road below them at a narrows that could easily be defended.

While both sides considered their next move the sheriff arrived. Riding up the slope to the mine, he ordered the men of the Merced Company to leave. As Frémont had expected they refused, citing the court ruling that allowed the seizing of any unoccupied mine. When the sheriff returned with warrants, three of the invaders laid down their arms, but the rest held their ground. That night Frémont gained a small advantage when several of his men managed to crawl through the enemy lines and get food and ammunition to the trapped men in the mine. But in the long run it achieved little. Frémont did not have enough men to break through and save the trapped men; the best he could do was keep his rifles trained on the enemy's back and force a stalemate where they could not move either. However, he had one hope, the arrival of the sheriff had told him that young Fox had gotten through.

On the fifth day Frémont's weary men heard the sound they had been waiting for, the distant tramp of feet and beat of drums. Five hundred state militiamen marched into the valley. Some of the hired gunmen, already disgusted with the affair, threw down their guns; and faced with the militia, the others were forced to withdraw, leaving Frémont in control of his mines again. For all the tension of the five-day siege and the random rifle fire, miraculously not a single life had been lost, but the Mariposa War, as the incident was called, with its army of hired gunmen, had proven one thing. Mining was big business now. The conflicts of the future would be between companies and big-money interests and the days of the solitary prospector with washbasin and pick were over.

For a few men the gold fever would never die. As early as 1856 some of these individual prospectors had wandered over the mountains to look for gold in Nevada. In 1857 and 1858 a few others drifted north to a new gold strike on the Fraser River in British Columbia. Then in 1859 a man named Harrison came into the Atwood Assay Office in Grass Valley with some mineral samples from Nevada.

"Any of the boys over that way having any luck?" the assayer asked.

"Henry Comstock and his partners have struck a pretty good vein of gold," Harrison explained, "but this funny-looking blue mineral keeps getting in their way. Comstock has been throwing it out, but a friend of mine suggested we have it assayed just to see if there might not be some gold in it after all."

The assayer promised a report in twenty-four hours.

The next morning Harrison returned. "Find any gold?" he asked.

"Gold? Sure I found some gold," the assayer gasped. "But the rest of that blue stuff is practically pure *silver!*"

By the end of that year most of the independent miners had disappeared over the mountains to the new rush on the Comstock in Nevada, taking with them the gamblers, dance-hall girls and adventurers, and leaving the California hills to settle down in the quiet peace of statehood and permanency. The mining towns were respectable now. Hangtown had changed its name to Placerville, Garrote preferred to be known as Groverdale, and a few of the smaller camps like Bidwell's Bar were already becoming ghost towns.

XIII

Postscript to Gold

JANUARY 24, 1848, WAS THE BEGINNING, BUT IT IS not possible to name a single day or even a year as the end of the gold rush. For some men the golden bubble burst violently in bitter disappointment; for others it deflated so slowly that one day they simply looked around them and saw that it was gone.

In 1862 a young writer, named Samuel Clemens, with a touch of mining fever came west to the big silver strike on the Comstock in Nevada; but he wasn't much of a miner and soon went to work as a reporter on Virginia City's *Territorial Enterprise*. Most of the readers enjoyed his robust humor, but some thought he went a little too far, so in time he decided it might be healthier to leave. He drifted on over the mountains to California to work on a San Francisco paper. Finally in the winter of 1864, he decided to get out of the city for a while and go up to Angel's Camp and visit Jim and Bill Gillis, who were mining on Jackass Hill.

There wasn't much to do in the winter evenings, so Clemens used to walk into town to the Angel's Hotel and listen as Ross Coon, the bartender, wove stories about the gold rush days. One of the stories about a jumping frog contest and how the miners ganged up on Jim Smiley and filled his frog with birdshot amused Clemens so much that he wrote it up and submitted it to a New York editor. "The Jumping Frog of Calaveras County" tickled the funnybone of a nation and launched the literary career of the new young writer,

Mark Twain. Later Clemens included more gold rush tales along with his own experiences in his book, *Roughing It.*

About this same time another writer, Francis Bret Harte, was winning acclaim on the West Coast. Harte had come to California as a youth in the gold rush days and worked variously as typesetter, printer, and an employee of the U.S. Mint while contributing articles to newspapers and literary magazines. By 1868 he had become the editor of the *Overland Monthly,* California's leading literary magazine. A close personal friend of Jessie and John Frémont and other notable figures, he was considered the leading writer on the coast. That year one of Harte's stories called "The Luck of Roaring Camp" was published in the *Overland Monthly.* It wasn't his first story, for he was a prolific writer, but it was one of his best. Years later of all Harte's voluminous writings, his tales of the gold rush, such as "The Luck of Roaring Camp," "The Outcasts of Poker Flat" and "Plain Language from Truthful James," were the ones that would be remembered.

Neither Harte nor Twain wrote of the gold rush as men who had actually lived those experiences but as storytellers who picked up the tales later and wove them into legends. Maybe that is a true test, that an event has slipped into history when its facts begin to be retold as legends. In that case, one could say the gold rush came to an end one winter day in 1864 when Mark Twain picked up his pen and wrote those nostalgic lines: "There was a feller here once by the name of Jim Smiley, in the winter of '49—or maybe it was the spring of '50 . . ."

The influence of the California gold rush had been felt around the world. It had made the United States one of the leading gold-producing nations, brought about the settlement of the Far West and added a new state to the Union. However, it had also created problems, some of which would extend almost to the turn of the century before they were completely solved.

For a decade California politics had been dominated by the Democratic party, with constant fighting between the Southern and the Tammany factions. In 1859 when this interparty struggle erupted in a duel between the Chief Justice of the State Supreme Court, David S. Terry, and former U.S. Senator David C. Broderick, in which the senator was killed, the long-suffering citizens had endured enough. In 1860 for the first time they voted overwhelmingly for a Republican party candidate, Abraham Lincoln; and with the exception of a few abortive Southern plots, the state remained loyal to the North throughout the Civil War, its vast mineral wealth going to help the Union cause. John C. Frémont was called back to the army to command the Union forces in the Department of the West, and with everyone united in the common war effort, the disgruntled southern counties finally gave up their plans for forming a separate territory.

Yet for all these uniting forces, the end of the war brought no solution for the major problem that had influenced California's destiny since the days of Cabrillo—her isolation from the rest of the world. In 1853 the Gadsden Purchase had been made with the idea of a transcontinental railway across a southern route, but for more than a decade the titanic job of laying two thousand miles of track seemed too much for anyone to attempt. However, the government awarded a mail franchise to Charles Butterfield, and by 1857 the jolting stages of his Overland Mail were carrying passengers and mail over this southern route in a journey of from seventeen to twenty-five days. Then in April, 1860, a boyish figure on a foam-flecked pony galloped into Placerville to throw off a packet of Pony Express Mail that had been posted in St. Joseph, Missouri, only ten days before.

For all its romance and color, the Pony Express was a

Father
Junipero Serra
Lieutenant
Colonel
John C. Frémont
William
Coleman
Captain
J.A. Sutter
Samuel
Brannan
President
James K. Polk
Men Who
Left Their Imprint
on California
General
M.G. Vallejo

financial failure, and a year later in 1861 it was made obsolete by the completion of the first telegraph line coast to coast. Now news could be transmitted within a day, but there still remained the problem of passengers and supplies. Out in California a young engineer, Theodore H. Judah, had revived the idea of a transcontinental railroad, only instead of the long-recommended southern route, he proposed to take it straight over the Sierras along the trails followed by the Donners and the men of forty-nine. Most people thought it such a wild idea that they started calling him "Crazy" Judah, and he could not get the backing of any bankers and financiers; but four merchants—Mark Hopkins, Collis Huntington, Charles Crocker and Leland Stanford, who had made good in the gold rush camps—gave the plan their backing. In July 1861, President Lincoln signed the Pacific Railroad Bill, and the Union Pacific started building west from Omaha and the Central Pacific, headed by the Big Four, as the merchants were to be called, started building east from Sacramento. The Sierra Nevadas proved a monumental obstacle but by hiring thousands of Chinese who were already working in the gold camps and importing thousands more from the Orient, the track was pushed over the mountains; and on May 10, 1869, the tracks of the two railways were joined at Promontory Point, Utah, ending California's isolation forever.

Oddly enough, the railway which had promised so much turned out to be something of a mixed blessing at first. For twenty years, California's economy had been geared to her isolation, and the sudden rush of cheap, eastern-produced goods upset local markets and called for readjustment. Moreover, once the transcontinental lines was finished, the Big Four turned to building tracks throughout California. Not only did they have a complete monopoly on transportation, but by virtue of the lands they acquired along their right-of-ways they soon became the biggest landowners in the state. Where twenty years before gold had dominated the life of the state, now some people told themselves bitterly the railroad controlled everything, and the 1870's were troubled years.

Not all of the unrest could be blamed on the railroad. In 1873 the entire nation suffered a depression brought about by the collapsing postwar boom. By 1875 its full force had hit the West Coast, and thousands of unemployed walked the streets of San Francisco, many willing to work for as little as a dollar a day. California, just starting to develop new industries, did not have jobs for them yet; and no matter how little these workers asked, there were now 116,000 Chinese in the state who would work for even less.

For over a decade the state legislature had been passing a variety of laws which attempted to discriminate against the Chinese, but invariably all had been thrown out of the higher courts as unconstitutional. Now the hatred formerly directed against the railroad turned to the Chinese as a threat to American labor. The slogan "The Chinese Must Go!" became a battle cry. In some towns there were bloody riots, and in San Francisco in 1877 unrest reached such a pitch that William Coleman was asked to summon another Committee of Safety and arm one thousand men to keep order on the streets. However, it could not be called a true vigilante action, for there were no trials, Coleman refused to allow his men to arm themselves with anything more lethal than pick handles, and after only a few skirmishes the group was disbanded again.

In 1878 the long-vexed people of California decided to attack their problem at the source and called for a convention to write a new state constitution. While the Constitution of 1850 had been a fine document, it had become outdated. It had given power to the legislators which had been abused, and it had made no provision for certain new problems which had arisen. The most notable changes in the new constitution completed the following year were a more equitable distribution of taxes, reduction of power of the legislature, creation of a Railroad Commission to curb the power of the rail monopoly, and a series of measures aimed at barring Chinese from employment in certain key industries.

As had been expected, the anti-Chinese measures were immediately declared unconstitutional by the Supreme Court, but they achieved their purpose. At last the legislators in Washington, D.C., were ready to admit that California did have a problem in its mounting Oriental population. Sad as it might seem, the quiet, industrious, willing Chinese worker, who had played such a part in building the West, had become a threat to the future of the American worker. In 1881 Congress passed an exclusion bill halting Chinese immigration for ten years. In 1892 this was extended another ten years by the Geary Act. In the early 1900's a combination of treaties and legislation made the exclusion permanent, and one of the unique problems rising from the gold rush had been solved.

The troubled seventies brought financial failure to a number of Californians, most notable among them Sam Brannan. Where others had turned their fortunes and interest to a more stable growth of the state, Brannan had never recovered from the gold fever. A born speculator, he had poured the million he had made from the early days of the gold rush back into new speculation. He spread his money too thin, mortgaged property as quickly as it was purchased and made unfortunate investments. He sunk a fortune in the unsuccessful promotion of a health resort at Calistoga and loaned money to Mexico to fight Maxmilian, which wasn't repaid. Among his investments was a winery, and it was soon said that he had become his own best customer. Creditors moved in on him, his wife Ann Eliza divorced him, and the remainder of his property was sold to meet her divorce settlement of a half-million dollars. In 1880 Brannan left

San Francisco penniless, a drunkard and outcast from both the Mormon Church and his family. After an unsuccessful attempt to start a colony in Sonora, Mexico, he drifted into temporary obscurity in Arizona and southern California.

Those qualities which had once made Brannan San Francisco's leading citizen were not going to let him go to a drunkard's grave. When Mexico eventually paid off its debt, he quit drinking, donned his pride and his best suit and returned to San Francisco, where he turned over every penny to his creditors. Then penniless again, he returned to southern California to die in poverty in 1889, the only mourner at his funeral the Mexican woman who had tended him through his last illness. "Gold from the American River!" Brannan had shouted as he ran down Montgomery Street that day in 1848, holding aloft his quinine bottle filled with yellow dust and setting off the great rush. Perhaps more than any other man, he represented the true spirit of those times, the feverish excitement that could drive a man to follow the golden bubble until it burst.

For all the troubles of the seventies, nothing could stop the new growth that the railroad also brought to the state. While Brannan chased his gold dream, pioneers such as John Bidwell and Pierson Reading had foreseen California's agricultural future and were experimenting with diversified crops on their ranches. However, until the coming of the railroad, California hides and wheat were the only agricultural products able to withstand the long voyage around the Horn. Now as the railroad opened markets in the East, other crops could be grown commercially. In 1873 Luther Tibbetts and his wife started the first plantings of the seedless navel orange from Brazil on their ranch near Riverside, and in 1877 William Wolfskill used the Southern Pacific to send the first shipment of California oranges to the East. Despite the high railroad charges he made a profit, and when a later shipment brought twenty-three thousand dollars there was a rush throughout southern California to plant citrus trees.

Though General Mariano Vallejo had suffered at the hands of the Americans in the Bear Flag Revolt and again in encounters with the Land Commission, his ability to adapt to changing conditions and his unflagging graciousness made him one of the most beloved citizens. With one of those grand gestures for which he was so noted he told people that whatever he had lost in land was more than made up by the greater wealth he possessed in his children. Indeed, all of his family prospered; his eldest son became a leading physician and his many daughters married well. The double wedding of two of his daughters to the two sons of Colonel Agoston Haraszthy, the noted Hungarian vintner, was one of the great social events of its day.

Colonel Haraszthy's importance to California was far greater than his ties with the Vallejo family. He purchased land from Vallejo at Sonoma and with his two sons started the Bella Vista vineyard that soon covered six thousand acres. As early as the mission days the Franciscan fathers' had grown wine grapes; and by 1842, Luis Vignes of Los Angeles was shipping his local wine and brandy throughout the state. But Haraszthy was one of the first to point out that while the "mission" grapes were of hardy stock their wine could not compete on the world market. In 1862 the state legislature authorized Haraszthy to return to Europe and bring back one hundred thousand cuttings of the Continent's best varieties of wine grapes. These cuttings, distributed by Haraszthy to California growers, became the foundation of the state's great wine industry.

Matching California's strides in agriculture in the 1880's and 1890's was the continuing development of her mineral resources. Though their output was less than that of the gold rush days, her gold mines continued to produce steadily, and new sources of mineral wealth were uncovered. One of the great discoveries made in 1880 was that the glaring wastes of Death Valley, across which Manly and the Briers had wandered so desperately, contained deposits of a valuable substance called borax. William Coleman, of Vigilante fame, was one of the leaders in developing the Pacific Coast Borax Company, whose fabled twenty-mule-team wagons were soon hauling this new product to market.

From 1860 to 1890 the production of whale oil was an important industry along the California coast, but the people of southern California had long known of another kind of oil that seeped from the ground. The Indians had used it to coat their baskets, and the citizens of Los Angeles had used it to tar the roofs of their adobe houses. The development of new drilling methods in Pennsylvania in the 1860's set off a rush to tap this new "black gold"; and by 1900, California's new oil wells were already producing four million barrels of petroleum a year.

Citrus, oil and climate were to develop southern California just as gold had developed the north. The railway was the first to advertise the mild climate and even offered prospective passengers return of their fare if the money was applied to the purchase of California land; but the big boom in population came in 1887 when the Atchison, Topeka and Santa Fe broke the Big Four's monopoly of almost twenty years by laying a track through to Los Angeles over the southern route discussed in the 1850's. The result was a price war that saw fares drop from one hundred twenty-five dollars to only one dollar.

In 1887, two hundred thousand people traveled by rail to California, double the number that had come west in the best year of the gold rush. Most headed for southern California where promoters met them with brass bands at dozens of new towns that had sprung up along the tracks, escorted them to elaborate barbecues and sold them land. A few of the subdivisions were frauds, such as one on the desert where ripe oranges were impaled on cactus plants and unwary easterners told that they were buying orange groves. When the boom burst many went home in disgust, but thousands stayed to form the backbone of the prosperous suburban towns that surround Los Angeles today. By 1900 California was no longer a frontier but a prosperous state with a population of over 1,400,400.

Yet even this was only a beginning. Within ten years the population would have increased another million, and it would keep on soaring. The completion of the Panama Canal in 1914 would furnish a new impetus to trade. The oil industry would become a behemoth. Other heavy industry would arrive. The years of World War II would bring a tremendous growth in aircraft production and shipbuilding, and the postwar years another wild population boom. By 1964 California would have become the most populous state and Los Angeles the third largest city in the Union.

On January 24, 1848, James Marshall had stooped to close a millrace and opened instead the floodgates to one of the greatest mass migrations the world had ever witnessed.

FURTHER SUGGESTED READING

Atherton, Gertrude. *Golden Gate Country*. Duell, Sloan & Pearce, New York, 1945.

Caughey, John W. and Laree. *California Heritage*. Ward Ritchie Press, Los Angeles, Calif., 1962.

Chalfant, W. A. *Death Valley*. Stanford University Press, Stanford, Calif., 1930.

Corle, Edwin. *The Royal Highway*. Bobbs-Merrill, New York, 1949.

Dickson, Samuel. *Tales of San Francisco*. Stanford University Press, Stanford, Calif., 1962.

Glasscock, C. B. *A Golden Highway*. A. L. Burt, New York, 1934.

Hulbert, Archer B. *Forty-Niners*. Little-Brown, Boston, Mass., 1949.

Jackson, Joseph H. *Anybody's Gold*. Appleton-Century, New York, 1941.

Marryat, Frank. *Mountains and Molehills*. Stanford University Press, Stanford, Calif., 1952.

O'Brien, Robert. *California Called Them*. McGraw-Hill, New York, 1951.

———. *This Is San Francisco*. McGraw-Hill, New York, 1948.

Paul, Rodman W. *California Gold*. Harvard University, Cambridge, Mass., 1947.

Stone, Irving. *Men to Match My Mountains*. Doubleday, Garden City, 1956.

Sunset Magazine, (Discovery Book). *Gold Rush Country*. Lane Publishing Co., Menlo Park, Calif., 1957.

Wells, Evelyn, and Peterson, Harry C. *The Forty-Niners*. Doubleday, New York, 1949.

Weston, Otheto. *Mother Lode Album*. Stanford University Press, Stanford, Calif., 1956.

Index

About the Authors

Bob Young was born on November 6, 1916, in the small northern California town of Chico. The family later moved to Sacramento, where he graduated from Sacramento Senior High and Sacramento Junior College.

Jan Young was born on March 6, 1916, in the small southern California desert town of Lancaster, where her father was publisher of the local weekly newspaper. Her family later moved to San Diego and then to south Pasadena, where she graduated from high school.

At the University of California at Los Angeles (UCLA) where Jan was an English major and Bob an economics major with an English minor, they found a common interest in writing. Bob transferred to the University of Nevada, and shortly after his graduation he and Jan were married.

Since Bob was unhappy at a desk job, they purchased an old pick-up truck and headed south. First came a fling at farming in Coachella Valley, then purchase of their first weekly newspaper, the *La Verne Leader*. They sold the newspaper in 1943 and Bob enlisted in the Army. He served overseas in New Guinea and the Philippine Islands, where he edited an Army newspaper. Meanwhile, Jan was kept busy at home with their sons Michael and Timothy.

After the war came another fling at farming, with Bob working as a newspaperman on another weekly paper, the *Desert Barnacle*. Later he was editor of the *Temple City Times*, then publisher and editor of his own paper, the *San Gabriel Sun*.

Deciding that their collaboration had been too long delayed, the Youngs sold the newspaper and turned to fulltime free-lance writing. Their first book, ACROSS THE TRACKS, was a Junior Literary Guild selection. This was followed by other novels for young people. Steeped in the history of California, they are now embarked on a number of non-fiction books dealing with the growth and development of their favorite state.